Descubra Juegos Gratis Online

Disponibles Aquí:

BestActivityBooks.com/FREEGAMES

5 CONSEJOS PARA EMPEZAR

1) CÓMO RESOLVER LAS SOPA DE LETRAS

Los rompecabezas tienen un formato clásico:

- Las palabras se ocultan sin espacios ni guiones,...
- Orientación: Las palabras pueden escribirse hacia delante, hacia atrás, hacia arriba, hacia abajo o en diagonal (pueden estar invertidas).
- Las palabras pueden superponerse o cruzarse.

2) APRENDIZAJE ACTIVO

Junto a cada palabra hay un espacio para anotar la traducción. Para fomentar un aprendizaje activo, un **DICCIONARIO** al final de esta edición te permitirá comprobar y ampliar tus conocimientos. Busca y anota las traducciones, encuéntralas en el puzzle y añádelas a tu vocabulario!

3) MARCAR LAS PALABRAS

Puedes inventar tu propio sistema de marcado. ¿Quizás ya usas uno? También puedes, por ejemplo, marcar las palabras difíciles de encontrar con una cruz, las que te gustan con una estrella, las nuevas con un triángulo, las raras con un diamante, etc.

4) ESTRUCTURAR EL APRENDIZAJE

Esta edición ofrece un **CUADERNO DE NOTAS** muy práctico al final del libro. En vacaciones, de viaje o en casa, podrás organizar fácilmente tus nuevos conocimientos sin necesidad de un segundo cuaderno!

5) ¿HABÉIS TERMINADO TODAS LAS PARRILLAS?

En las últimas páginas de este libro, en la sección **DESAFÍO FINAL**, encontrarás un juego gratis!

¡Rápido y sencillo! Echa un vistazo a nuestra colección de libros de actividades para tu próximo momento de diversión y aprendizaje, ¡a sólo un clic de distancia!

Encuentre su próximo reto en:

BestActivityBooks.com/MiProximoLibro

En sus marcas, listos, ¡Ya!

¿Sabías que hay unas 7.000 lenguas diferentes en el mundo? Las palabras son preciosas.

Nos encantan los idiomas y hemos trabajado duro para crear libros de la más alta calidad para tí. ¿Nuestros ingredientes?

Una selección de temas adecuados para el aprendizaje, tres buenas porciones de entretenimiento, y luego añadimos una cucharada de palabras difíciles y una pizca de palabras raras. Los servimos con cariño y máxima diversión para que puedas resolver los mejores juegos de palabras y te diviertas aprendiendo!

Tu opinión es esencial. Puedes participar activamente en el éxito de este libro dejándonos un comentario. Nos encantaría saber qué es lo que más le ha gustado de esta edición.

Aquí hay un enlace rápido a tu página de pedidos:

BestBooksActivity.com/Opiniones50

Gracias por tu ayuda y diviértete!

Todo el equipo

1 - Arqueología

```
Y R E T S Y M K Q A F V C P R
T E U U H K P L I H O R I R E
I M A E T H I U Y M R J V O S
U D R R Z O Y M D D G C I F E
Q P E G S E N O B M O T L E A
I N V L S M N B L D T F I S R
T F U N K N O W N E T O Z S C
N P Z K Q D I C A S E S A O H
A U W D S I T F N C N S T R E
T E M P L E A G A E V I I D R
R E L I C K U D L N W L O S N
Y A B X O Q L B Y D D U N N G
E X P E R T A P S A U E U D X
H C Q P F A V L I N E Q J F E
J M V Q Q T E M S T C E J B O
```

ANALYSIS
ANTIQUITY
YEARS
CIVILIZATION
DESCENDANT
UNKNOWN
TEAM
ERA
EVALUATION
EXPERT

FOSSIL
BONES
RESEARCHER
MYSTERY
OBJECTS
FORGOTTEN
PROFESSOR
RELIC
TEMPLE
TOMB

2 - Granja #2

```
F G G F C O R N L G L B M O Q
A V W A X D S T Z D A P E R B
B M D R E H P E H S M A A C C
F T Y M W E N V H B B N D H G
V P E E H S O I Q B O I O A T
W E L R L X I H I B Q M W R F
W H E A T R T E D D V A K D K
F R U I T Y A E A H Q L J E I
T L L A M A G B E L J S I D S
V R J K S H I V Y L K S X O Y
A S A W X R R M Y P T O F U Z
O Z C C G E R O W Z B A R N Y
Q T K W T M I L K C U D O O F
A J A E V O V E G E T A B L E
I H G A Z I R H Q M C P L U P
```

FARMER	LLAMA
ANIMALS	CORN
BARLEY	SHEEP
BEEHIVE	SHEPHERD
FOOD	DUCK
LAMB	MEADOW
FRUIT	IRRIGATION
BARN	TRACTOR
ORCHARD	WHEAT
MILK	VEGETABLE

3 - Mueble

```
M A T T R E S S D E S K R J C
N C E A E S N I A T R U C C L
J O V R S A O C S H E L V E S
M U I M S C I R H E S D A M R
X C L O E K H W C A B L F B E
F H L I R O S W N B I D T H T
C U I R D O U K E M E R H V R
K W T E S B C S B P L D A O O
C D H O D Q R R L A M P T M F
O L L S N Z A U O F I E O I M
M I R R O R M G A B N L U N O
M A R M C H A I R S X U V S C
A Z J W A V J G Y P I L L O W
H F T F Y W Z N M P J P C B K
H J Z B K W K U H H D R L Z O
```

RUG	DESK
PILLOW	MIRROR
ARMOIRE	BOOKCASE
BENCH	SHELVES
BED	FUTON
CUSHIONS	HAMMOCK
MATTRESS	LAMP
CURTAINS	CHAIR
DRESSER	ARMCHAIR
COMFORTERS	COUCH

4 - Aviones

```
C  S  L  W  P  A  T  B  E  Z  S  E  C  X  V
O  R  K  R  A  T  U  A  N  X  H  F  O  P  H
G  I  E  Y  S  M  R  L  G  H  J  D  K  P  F
E  A  B  W  S  O  B  L  I  U  M  Y  W  N  V
W  A  Y  S  E  S  U  O  N  X  U  F  Q  G  R
A  M  R  O  N  P  L  O  E  Y  T  H  D  M  N
N  L  O  A  G  H  E  N  E  G  O  R  D  Y  H
C  E  T  N  E  E  N  G  Y  H  E  I  G  H  T
X  U  S  I  R  R  C  I  R  F  R  W  O  C  D
O  F  I  W  T  E  E  S  D  L  D  H  Y  M  U
E  P  H  S  W  U  E  E  C  B  Y  S  N  I  O
Z  W  C  I  Y  Y  D  D  L  A  N  D  I  N  G
I  H  V  W  F  S  R  E  L  L  E  P  O  R  P
S  Y  D  I  R  E  C  T  I  O  N  N  S  H  Z
A  D  V  E  N  T  U  R  E  P  I  L  O  T  O
```

AIR	BALLOON
ALTITUDE	PROPELLERS
HEIGHT	HYDROGEN
LANDING	HISTORY
ATMOSPHERE	ENGINE
ADVENTURE	PASSENGER
SKY	PILOT
FUEL	CREW
DIRECTION	TURBULENCE
DESIGN	

5 - Tipos de Cabello

```
F  J  L  E  J  Y  J  J  K  R  L  O  Q  E  M
I  I  P  H  Q  L  M  J  S  V  Q  X  Z  A  F
Z  D  L  A  B  Z  R  B  T  W  C  D  C  K  O
A  R  E  V  L  I  S  L  S  O  F  T  C  S  U
R  Y  L  R  U  C  J  W  S  R  B  O  U  J  P
W  H  O  J  G  R  T  E  W  E  Z  D  R  O  Y
A  V  E  V  N  F  Z  G  K  K  F  L  L  C  D
Y  M  T  A  O  S  H  I  N  Y  W  G  S  Q  D
T  H  I  N  L  B  R  O  W  N  P  A  R  Z  X
U  B  H  J  N  T  R  O  H  S  S  I  V  A  W
B  L  W  K  C  I  H  T  B  D  T  B  G  Y  Y
L  A  R  E  D  O  K  Y  E  I  C  O  X  O  P
O  C  V  X  W  G  Q  S  P  A  F  B  B  K  J
N  K  R  T  Y  X  Y  G  B  R  A  I  D  E  D
D  W  H  B  I  W  D  S  X  B  X  A  G  P  G
```

WHITE	WAVY
SHINY	SILVER
BALD	CURLY
SHORT	CURLS
THIN	BLOND
GRAY	HEALTHY
THICK	DRY
LONG	SOFT
BROWN	BRAIDED
BLACK	BRAIDS

6 - Ética

```
D V A L U E S Q M I D T R R P
K B V F T Y S C J N I O E A O
D M Q G C T Z J U T P L S K A
K E Z S W I K V P E L E P I C
V Y Z I F N H T Y G O R E N O
G M S I L A E R U R M A C D M
W O P T I M I S M I A N T N P
D I M W S U E I I T T C F E A
I P S Y A H E C U Y I E U S S
G S I D H N I D N R C M L S S
N V U N O I T A R E P O O C I
I M R Y W M W T M P I X G E O
T Y T S E N O H Q Z U T M R N
Y E L B A N O S A E R F A O R
X H A B Y H P O S O L I H P K
```

ALTRUISM
KINDNESS
COMPASSION
COOPERATION
DIGNITY
DIPLOMATIC
PHILOSOPHY
HONESTY
HUMANITY

INTEGRITY
OPTIMISM
PATIENCE
REASONABLE
REALISM
RESPECTFUL
WISDOM
TOLERANCE
VALUES

7 - Ciencia Ficción

```
I M A G I N A R Y X A L A G R
U S S E W E X P L O S I O N E
G U T M O H E L C A R O H K A
Y O U K R X L X R V G S J A L
C I A L L T M S T C Y S B T I
I R X I D G C K Z R Z Z I O S
T E C H N O L O G Y E N A M T
S T F D O J K O L B J M Z I I
I S I U I P G B U G L I E C C
R Y R T S S L V S N W F Y M G
U M E O U T T A M E N I C V H
T E A P L O Y A N C M W I W Y
U P B I L B P D N E X Q P U L
F L E A I O K Q Z T T Z U Z A
K I N L V R F A N T A S T I C
```

ATOMIC   IMAGINARY
CINEMA   BOOKS
DISTANT   MYSTERIOUS
EXPLOSION   WORLD
EXTREME   ORACLE
FANTASTIC   PLANET
FIRE   REALISTIC
FUTURISTIC   ROBOTS
GALAXY   TECHNOLOGY
ILLUSION   UTOPIA

8 - Granja #1

```
D K V J E E B Y T T S S R C C
O G P Y R X F A V N V E K R O
G O E P U G M M K W Z E R O W
E S M L T W V W Q S Z D J W C
P A R Q L A N D M O O S F E H
F U E G U Z C A W O C A T L I
A Y A H C Y K I E E C N E F C
F E R T I L I Z E R I A A E K
V N A O R H W B R H K G L A E
G O P A G N A C R I Q T G F N
F H C C A R T K M V C A O H Q
Q I G C U E E S R O H E A D M
E Y E F Q J R P C R K I T N C
R Q H L D O N K E Y L G W U J
Z D R T D O J S Q W C I Y J Y
```

BEE	CAT
AGRICULTURE	HAY
WATER	HONEY
RICE	DOG
DONKEY	CHICKEN
HORSE	SEEDS
GOAT	CALF
FIELD	LAND
CROW	COW
FERTILIZER	FENCE

9 - Camping

```
R  R  R  J  Q  H  I  U  K  B  C  F  K  R  R
L  X  F  S  G  U  X  N  O  O  M  I  Y  A  F
E  T  S  N  Z  N  U  R  S  S  A  P  M  O  C
P  C  S  Q  X  T  T  E  I  E  X  A  O  R  I
H  S  A  L  K  I  L  T  K  Z  C  M  L  K  D
N  M  M  B  A  N  Y  N  R  A  R  T  T  E  D
P  L  Y  L  I  G  M  A  Y  E  O  N  A  C  N
X  H  O  A  P  N  B  L  S  K  E  H  N  Z  R
M  O  U  N  T  A  I  N  M  A  F  S  I  L  H
A  D  V  E  N  T  U  R  E  L  O  D  M  L  A
E  Q  U  I  P  M  E  N  T  Q  R  E  A  S  M
R  O  P  E  R  U  T  A  N  L  E  E  L  V  M
I  H  A  T  W  O  T  O  I  R  S  Y  S  X  O
F  K  U  A  H  Q  Q  K  M  C  T  P  U  Y  C
S  I  N  Z  N  J  L  S  F  S  O  J  X  F  K
```

ANIMALS	FIRE
ADVENTURE	HAMMOCK
TREES	INSECT
FOREST	LAKE
COMPASS	LANTERN
CABIN	MOON
CANOE	MAP
HUNTING	MOUNTAIN
ROPE	NATURE
EQUIPMENT	HAT

10 - Fruta

```
Q O D A C O V A N A N A B C G
D G T M T C S M M C E V I O R
R N P I N E A P P L E J P C A
C A L E M O N S S B Q G M O P
R M S Q L O W R U D F G G N E
M M E P M D U Q T S C X Z U A
N J I P B G Q P A P A Y A T P
F E T C Q E G N A R O R C V P
P H C A E P R S X Y C R H B L
K E B T O C I R P A F E E Q E
N X A V A U G B Y M L B R M P
M Y C R X R K I W I C L R G J
L Z I X Q Z I Y C M Q S Y N B
Y P G O X L R N O L E M K U M
C Z C O W J L N E Z E Y Q C B
```

AVOCADO	APPLE
APRICOT	PEACH
BERRY	MELON
CHERRY	ORANGE
COCONUT	NECTARINE
RASPBERRY	PAPAYA
GUAVA	PEAR
KIWI	PINEAPPLE
LEMON	BANANA
MANGO	GRAPE

11 - Geología

```
O U H K A W J O O C R Z X O L
C R Y S T A L S V O D U N F X
C O N T I N E N T R E Y A L C
F J X N G D H S L A R E N I M
Q A L X M E R N B L S R O S U
A U F T C X Y N X F T Y I S I
L U A Z V D X S O W A S S O C
C G Y R K U U C E Q L T O F L
T E Z H T L A S M R A O R N A
W E L J C Z E D Z G C N E I C
E K A U Q H T R A E T E B R V
A X V B D V A R L H I A K F U
J V A V B N L K Q N T X C F O
J G F J Y J P P P P E E K I F
K S C A V E R N R C M J M J D
```

ACID	STALACTITE
CALCIUM	FOSSIL
LAYER	GEYSER
CAVERN	LAVA
CONTINENT	PLATEAU
CORAL	MINERALS
CRYSTALS	STONE
QUARTZ	SALT
EROSION	EARTHQUAKE

12 - Álgebra

```
F  M  H  E  D  W  Y  Z  M  T  N  Q  M  F  V
E  A  W  T  X  U  O  E  S  B  O  U  D  A  Y
F  Q  L  S  O  P  P  R  S  O  I  A  D  C  P
D  N  U  S  P  V  O  O  H  M  T  N  N  T  A
J  U  S  A  E  L  Z  N  C  G  C  T  K  O  R
K  M  A  C  T  Q  M  Y  E  T  A  I  T  R  E
S  B  S  A  I  I  F  I  B  N  R  T  F  A  N
O  E  Y  D  N  W  O  K  X  T  T  Y  F  E  T
L  R  F  P  I  J  I  N  U  Q  B  G  O  N  H
U  A  I  I  F  W  E  Y  I  E  U  P  R  I  E
T  S  L  A  N  V  A  C  E  W  S  H  M  L  S
I  L  P  K  I  M  A  T  R  I  X  P  U  Z  I
O  M  M  F  R  A  C  T  I  O  N  Y  L  V  S
N  O  I  S  I  V  I  D  M  A  R  G  A  I  D
S  Y  S  J  K  P  R  O  B  L  E  M  Q  Q  K
```

QUANTITY	INFINITE
ZERO	LINEAR
DIAGRAM	MATRIX
DIVISION	NUMBER
EQUATION	PARENTHESIS
EXPONENT	PROBLEM
FACTOR	SUBTRACTION
FALSE	SIMPLIFY
FORMULA	SOLUTION
FRACTION	

13 - Plantas

```
R V G H R D F V N I F W N Z D
O E R A L P A O W V B E R R Y
O G B T H A J L R Y X C O R N
T E H T X R E P N E D R A G A
L T S B A M B O O K S S O M T
Q A C Y O T R E E A U T B I O
O T T X I T N D V M T N U Z B
F I A G Y X F Y M K C J S G Z
U O P N D R C O O P A V H I H
U N U F L O R A L A C J A U M
R M Z P R E Z I L I T R E F R
W T H Z T L H W V N A E B E D
I N Z F P E K Y M J F G F Z I
D K M S S A R G Y H H W E Q J
P E T A L F F L O W E R I G M
```

BUSH
TREE
BAMBOO
BERRY
FOREST
BOTANY
CACTUS
FERTILIZER
FLOWER
FLORA

FOLIAGE
BEAN
IVY
GRASS
LEAF
GARDEN
MOSS
PETAL
ROOT
VEGETATION

14 - Suministros de Arte

```
W Q X T S R O L O C R E T A W
U D T L K B K W B R H U B K K
I P Y H Y M O P I E U L G M E
S H S C A B K A V A Z I G W L
A C R Y L I C I U T W O X K M
E Y E S C H K N I I V P R C K
D R P F V O Q T K V V E T Y R
I C A M G E L S L I C N E P B
A J P S L O I O C T C Z W H X
X D I E E C W T R Y A T A T T
G Z Z H S R H X Q S M G T A Y
N T C S A N X A Q V E M E B Z
W G S U E C U M I Y R W R L S
P B B R C B W V A R A O M E S
P J B B D P A S T E L S X N U
```

OIL	CREATIVITY
ACRYLIC	IDEAS
WATERCOLORS	PENCILS
WATER	TABLE
CLAY	PAPER
ERASER	PASTELS
EASEL	GLUE
CAMERA	PAINTS
BRUSHES	CHAIR
COLORS	INK

15 - Negocio

```
M O N E Y N M P U C O S T W M
E M P L O Y E R T R G U H F G
E C O N O M I C S M Y F S X S
M E R C H A N D I S E L A S O
U J G D S I N V E S T M E N T
D G M X W H C T C L E O B O J
Z C T R L C O Q I C M G C I X
Z A B D C K A P F J P R L T S
X R C Q I U W N F E L J B C T
S E X A T S R A O F O I C A N
T E G D U B C R Y P Y M C S L
K R A P A P X O E K E M N N C
C O M P A N Y G U N E M N A G
F I N A N C E Z F N C R I R E
F A C T O R Y W A K T Y E T M
```

CAREER	TAXES
COST	INVESTMENT
DISCOUNT	MERCHANDISE
MONEY	CURRENCY
ECONOMICS	OFFICE
EMPLOYEE	BUDGET
EMPLOYER	SHOP
COMPANY	JOB
FACTORY	TRANSACTION
FINANCE	SALE

16 - Jardín

```
W R O J P F Q I B G B T W N E
L R E W O L F G W U O R E X W
K J E E R T Q N R L S S E K A
Z E H C C G A R D E N H D P W
O T B A H O C L G V W C S H U
V S E R M J R O R O A P O N D
R E N R K M P C H H L N X K F
B T C E Z P O E H S S A R G V
L Q H T C Y G C Y A S O I L F
T V O O L W T E K A R V B O E
A H K J I J K O M R Y D L B N
Z Y W I E N U A X P P F T S C
N Y M I D M A T O C E G L N E
T R A M P O L I N E G A R A G
O W Y J H O S E J X B V N P S
```

BUSH
TREE
BENCH
LAWN
POND
FLOWER
GARAGE
HAMMOCK
GRASS
ORCHARD

GARDEN
WEEDS
HOSE
SHOVEL
PORCH
RAKE
SOIL
TERRACE
TRAMPOLINE
FENCE

17 - Países #2

```
N  C  T  D  E  N  M  A  R  K  R  H  O  Q  F
A  I  S  E  N  O  D  N  I  X  W  D  X  O  R
U  F  S  A  I  L  A  R  T  S  U  A  X  G  A
L  Y  U  X  A  I  R  Y  S  E  B  S  O  B  N
A  N  D  G  R  B  L  M  J  A  P  A  N  Y  C
G  G  A  X  K  Q  J  W  E  A  L  O  P  R  E
U  R  N  X  U  O  L  P  K  X  H  G  V  U  E
T  S  E  P  S  R  A  A  O  X  I  D  D  S  T
R  S  S  E  L  L  O  I  L  E  W  C  M  S  H
O  P  H  N  C  A  S  R  S  B  F  X  O  I  I
P  C  H  L  K  E  Q  T  Q  Y  A  K  H  A  O
J  A  M  A  I  C  A  S  G  P  Y  N  B  W  P
I  R  E  L  A  N  D  U  W  S  S  J  I  Q  I
U  G  A  N  D  A  C  A  V  M  D  A  R  A  A
F  Z  G  W  P  A  K  I  S  T  A  N  Q  F  C
```

ALBANIA	JAPAN
AUSTRALIA	LAOS
AUSTRIA	MEXICO
DENMARK	PAKISTAN
ETHIOPIA	PORTUGAL
FRANCE	RUSSIA
GREECE	SYRIA
INDONESIA	SUDAN
IRELAND	UKRAINE
JAMAICA	UGANDA

18 - Números

```
D  N  E  V  E  S  G  F  J  C  Z  Z  E  N  D
N  E  E  T  X  I  S  I  T  T  Q  E  D  F  O
T  E  C  H  K  Q  E  F  H  B  A  T  T  D  S
W  T  W  I  S  I  X  T  H  V  K  R  K  D  T
E  H  Z  O  M  F  N  E  E  T  R  U  O  F  H
L  G  S  B  N  A  N  E  I  T  B  G  S  T  I
V  I  T  L  Z  N  L  N  G  W  F  P  L  H  R
E  E  Q  W  C  O  K  F  H  E  O  S  M  R  T
P  N  D  Q  O  C  D  I  T  N  U  Z  I  E  E
V  J  Q  C  N  K  V  V  P  T  R  K  E  E  E
N  C  K  M  M  D  V  E  Z  Y  K  I  D  R  N
N  I  N  E  N  I  N  E  T  E  E  N  N  W  O
S  E  V  E  N  T  E  E  N  Y  S  D  R  E  T
P  E  K  Q  U  S  T  N  G  L  O  Y  E  Q  F
G  H  Q  J  V  A  J  H  F  G  A  A  V  W  X
```

FOURTEEN	TWELVE
ZERO	TWO
FIVE	NINE
FOUR	EIGHT
DECIMAL	FIFTEEN
NINETEEN	SIX
EIGHTEEN	SEVEN
SIXTEEN	THIRTEEN
SEVENTEEN	THREE
TEN	TWENTY

19 - Física

```
F V Z M D R S N X N D S A B G
J R F P A W P U Y H E W C K R
V A E U A G E I F W N T C I A
M E R Q L O N D Q Z S M E B V
B L A I U J I E O T I M L Z I
C C T E M E G X T G T A E A T
H U O L R I N E H I Y S R O Y
A N M U O B E C F E S S A P V
O L G C F G V W Y G V M T A E
S E L E C T R O N Z A I I R L
Z S J L K O N E H E V S O T O
N M Y O P G Y B T I G U N I C
C H E M I C A L G E K T R C I
M E C H A N I C S S L Y W L T
U N I V E R S A L S Y S F E Y
```

ACCELERATION
ATOM
CHAOS
DENSITY
ELECTRON
FORMULA
FREQUENCY
GAS
GRAVITY
MAGNETISM

MASS
MECHANICS
MOLECULE
ENGINE
NUCLEAR
PARTICLE
CHEMICAL
UNIVERSAL
VELOCITY

20 - Belleza

```
S  L  I  O  H  C  Z  E  Y  E  F  V  H  J  F
D  T  A  B  V  L  S  L  P  L  R  G  C  H  E
C  P  Y  L  S  C  E  E  K  E  A  O  B  S  M
U  H  C  L  C  A  E  G  P  G  G  A  L  R  V
R  O  O  Q  I  R  Y  A  Y  A  R  E  Z  O  H
L  T  S  J  T  S  F  N  E  N  A  T  F  S  C
S  O  M  B  A  T  T  T  O  C  N  I  K  S  D
I  G  E  S  S  Q  S  Y  N  E  C  G  C  I  I
X  E  T  E  O  A  C  O  X  E  E  Z  I  C  D
A  N  I  R  O  R  R  I  M  J  C  N  T  S  H
S  I  C  V  P  A  U  I  R  N  A  S  S  S  A
R  C  S  I  M  C  A  X  A  B  R  V  P  D  J
M  Q  Q  C  A  S  K  Y  H  F  G  U  I  M  P
Q  C  N  E  H  A  V  D  C  Y  K  E  L  E  T
C  K  V  S  S  M  M  A  K  E  U  P  N  Q  B
```

OILS	PHOTOGENIC
SCENT	FRAGRANCE
SHAMPOO	GRACE
COLOR	MAKEUP
COSMETICS	SKIN
ELEGANCE	LIPSTICK
ELEGANT	CURLS
CHARM	MASCARA
MIRROR	SERVICES
STYLIST	SCISSORS

21 - Países #1

```
N I T A L Y B L H H T B E I U
I F H J K Y J M R Y S E L N Y
C I P H O N D U R A S L I D U
A J C H N A W O U W H G B I L
R D W O I Q R W D R F I Y A M
A T H H A L Y G L O B U A B T
G U D E P P I P E N N M R E R
U M G F S A D P Y N A M R E G
A T R I Z A N Z P L T P Y G E
Z M O Q R V V A L I S I T G J
W D D H Q A Y H M L N O N F I
B R A Z I L H E H A S E O A J
Q A U P O L A N D M X U S Y Y
H O C C O R O M C A N A D A I
A L E U Z E N E V V Z M T Z C
```

GERMANY
ARGENTINA
BELGIUM
BRAZIL
CANADA
ECUADOR
EGYPT
SPAIN
PHILIPPINES
HONDURAS

INDIA
ITALY
LIBYA
MALI
MOROCCO
NICARAGUA
NORWAY
PANAMA
POLAND
VENEZUELA

22 - Mitología

```
B H E A V E N C D J Y Z H E L
M E D X I J H U I E I E L E I
F R H Q Y P R L S A K K J A G
D Y V A Q R E T A L I C Z S H
S T Z W V O O U S O R E H T T
U I H E L I N R T U A B C H N
R L T G X R O E E S R E W U I
S A N E R R I R R Y C L C N N
U T I G L A T R O M H I R D G
I R R N P W A V T Z E E E E B
R O Y E D N E G E L T F A R U
C M B V N E R J F K Y S T W F
G M A E J G C F W Z P F U Y I
P I L R S U T R K J E Q R U O
M O N S T E R H Z W G S E T Q
```

ARCHETYPE
JEALOUSY
HEAVEN
BEHAVIOR
CREATION
BELIEFS
CREATURE
CULTURE
DISASTER
STRENGTH

WARRIOR
HERO
IMMORTALITY
LABYRINTH
LEGEND
MONSTER
MORTAL
LIGHTNING
THUNDER
REVENGE

23 - Ecología

```
V O L U N T E E R S D T N F S
T V G U P L A N T S I B A R U
Q N J I C U O F L I V P T F S
F W F I C T I P X D E Y U B T
S F U E I C X E V J R Y R V A
P Y L A V I V R U S S X A E I
E O C O F B U U I E I G L G N
C D M P R A Q T R C T L T E A
I Z G N J A U A R R Y O V T B
E M A R I N E N Y U M B A A L
S D R O U G H T A O A A R T E
H A B I T A T B P S R L I I G
X I A U L I P W B E S P E O C
I T B V G E Y O G R H E T N Q
H L W W G C L I M A T E Y F S
```

CLIMATE
DIVERSITY
SPECIES
FAUNA
FLORA
GLOBAL
HABITAT
MARINE
NATURAL
NATURE

MARSH
PLANTS
RESOURCES
DROUGHT
SUSTAINABLE
SURVIVAL
VARIETY
VEGETATION
VOLUNTEERS

24 - Casa

```
W F J F A U C E T Z K B R I F
C A U J K Q W G Q K F B O D Y
G I L L G N I A D O O R O M O
Z A W L E C N R C E O Y F N B
X Q R Q A R D A T T I C C J F
S Y R D D U O G R H A W Z B I
K N Q B E G W O V D S K L R R
U I Y S O N G J H W Z Y A O E
F U T N E M E S A B R Y M O P
U S D C B I R F L O O R P M L
E L Z A H B W B S H R A B Z A
T H G S G E C N E F R R E X C
S H O W E R N J W F I B Y T E
U B L C E O I C A Q M I P M Q
B E D R O O M N U S K L Z C I
```

RUG
ATTIC
LIBRARY
FIREPLACE
KITCHEN
BEDROOM
SHOWER
BROOM
MIRROR
GARAGE

FAUCET
GARDEN
LAMP
WALL
FLOOR
DOOR
BASEMENT
ROOF
FENCE
WINDOW

25 - Salud y Bienestar #2

```
C E S Q I L H E A L T H Y S R
D A W E I G H T P X E F H S E
I X L D E N S S E R T S O D C
S T N O I T C E F N I I S J O
E G I O R N I M A T I V P M V
A G X L T I T F C S V H I L E
S E D B D P E T D Y W O T P R
E R U I I X N T W A O D A Y Y
C R H Y G R E E I O U R L G G
X V X N R E G I J T Z F V R R
D P Z F H I S D Y R E L K E E
H Y G I E N E T K K Z P D L N
M A S S A G E T I M X A P L E
M A Q Z X H C Y M O T A N A R
N U T R I T I O N V N S D G R
```

ALLERGY
ANATOMY
APPETITE
CALORIE
DIET
DIGESTION
ENERGY
DISEASE
STRESS
GENETICS

HYGIENE
HOSPITAL
INFECTION
MASSAGE
NUTRITION
WEIGHT
RECOVERY
HEALTHY
BLOOD
VITAMIN

26 - Selva Tropical

```
S  R  E  S  T  O  R  A  T  I  O  N  A  I  P
D  U  I  W  J  M  D  Q  L  Q  I  J  M  N  R
R  L  R  D  Y  U  Z  K  O  K  R  U  P  D  E
I  E  L  V  T  C  O  E  J  M  E  N  H  I  S
B  L  A  C  I  N  A  T  O  B  F  G  I  E  E
Y  B  Y  G  S  V  T  C  I  T  U  L  B  E  R
X  A  T  Z  R  R  A  J  L  H  G  E  I  N  V
B  U  I  K  E  E  E  L  B  I  E  S  A  O  A
V  L  N  A  V  S  S  S  O  M  M  D  N  U  T
O  A  U  H  I  D  P  Y  P  E  H  A  S  S  I
H  V  M  I  D  H  E  W  L  E  F  N  T  U  O
E  P  M  K  N  S  C  Y  M  U  C  J  I  E  N
C  L  O  U  D  S  I  X  E  R  U  T  A  N  G
K  Q  C  C  W  V  E  M  A  M  M  A  L  S  L
Z  N  Q  B  Z  J  S  I  N  S  E  C  T  S  Y
```

AMPHIBIANS	NATURE
BOTANICAL	CLOUDS
CLIMATE	BIRDS
COMMUNITY	PRESERVATION
DIVERSITY	REFUGE
SPECIES	RESPECT
INDIGENOUS	RESTORATION
INSECTS	JUNGLE
MAMMALS	SURVIVAL
MOSS	VALUABLE

27 - Colores

```
A C Y E Z W B F W L V V O P G
K Z Y X J H G E P C V U R U E
C Y U A O I X Q V W J R A R O
C J W R N T Y E L L O W N P Y
M S U S E E U L B I L U G L C
B R O W N S G G Y W O Q E E H
M A G E N T A R E D G Q S V B
B D K A Z L S B R A I R J K P
M S Y D G Q F L G U D B E Z N
S Y C J B P A A A U N E E E E
E U K E H B E C M L I I Y A N
P V I O L E T K B L Y G P D C
I R B L Q B N F V V Y E K W T
A T C C R I M S O N I Z T H B
P I N K C D F U C H S I A G Y
```

YELLOW	MAGENTA
BLUE	BROWN
AZURE	ORANGE
BEIGE	BLACK
WHITE	PURPLE
CRIMSON	RED
CYAN	PINK
FUCHSIA	SEPIA
GREY	GREEN
INDIGO	VIOLET

28 - Adjetivos #1

```
F A H P D K H A A B I A A V V
R V Z T Q N B M R L N T C A O
V X O I I R Y B O H N T T L P
J H T H Y W A I M U O R I U Z
M T S E N O H T A G C A V A F
H N H A I L N I T E E C E B W
M A B G B S I O I S N T K L A
G T Q E I S T U C K T I R E M
U R K N U R O S K L Y V A E H
I O G E H V B L B E Y E D G A
W P N R E D O M U Q D Y V R J
F M O O V Z Q S R T L O Q A Q
I I X U X S M B N K E U M L P
X L C S U O I R E S J N N T U
P E R F E C T B B L L G T U Q
```

ABSOLUTE	IMPORTANT
ACTIVE	INNOCENT
AMBITIOUS	YOUNG
AROMATIC	SLOW
ATTRACTIVE	MODERN
BRIGHT	DARK
HUGE	PERFECT
GENEROUS	HEAVY
LARGE	SERIOUS
HONEST	VALUABLE

29 - Familia

```
I O E A U U A X X T B V M E D
R I Q N O S D N A R G O N E O
E O K C J U Z T W E K G H T M
H I W E H P E N C N I E C E O
T J E S F F D H J N R C G C T
A N L T J B R O T H E R R H H
F U C O M A T E R N A L A I E
D H N R D A U G H T E R N L R
N S U T C H I L D R E N D D E
A M I S C O U S I N F E M H H
R J U S B K B Y Y M I X O O T
G U O C T A Q N B G W O T O A
H K L L H E N V N O Y D H D F
R P E O N U R D L I H C E L S
W I A T T Q M V B M G H R T U
```

GRANDMOTHER	MATERNAL
GRANDFATHER	GRANDSON
ANCESTOR	CHILD
WIFE	CHILDREN
SISTER	FATHER
BROTHER	COUSIN
DAUGHTER	NIECE
CHILDHOOD	NEPHEW
MOTHER	AUNT
HUSBAND	UNCLE

30 - Disciplinas Científicas

```
A S T R O N O M Y G N I A Q T
G X L S K D D F M E E M R V H
S Y O I B A D Y O O U M C S X
C S O U N Y G R T L R U H O E
H C X W Y G V T A O N A C P
E I G D G O U S N G L O E I H
M N C E O L F I A Y O L O O Y
I A U O L O D M S T G O L L S
S H B T O C Y E O T Y G O O I
T C I D R E D H F Z I Y G G O
R E O G O I L C N P J C Y Y L
Y M L B E A T O K W L O S I O
S L O S T J W I B O T A N Y G
F D G W E F V B O K M A X R Y
Z J Y J M N L Q P N P Y A K M
```

ANATOMY

ARCHAEOLOGY

ASTRONOMY

BIOLOGY

BIOCHEMISTRY

BOTANY

ECOLOGY

PHYSIOLOGY

GEOLOGY

IMMUNOLOGY

LINGUISTICS

MECHANICS

METEOROLOGY

NEUROLOGY

NUTRITION

CHEMISTRY

SOCIOLOGY

31 - Cocina

```
A X H Q G K A L H D V R H F Y
B V H B N I K P A N E V O Y W
V H P G E N H J R D Z N Q B O
T E D R W L O U D O O F Y K G
S P I C E S D G N A N C I G C
Q I B M T O E A T U L M G R F
F C I Q S K F E L T T E K V R
R E F R I G E R A T O R Y S E
H R X J Y R L S M T H Q S K E
C H O P S T I C K S V G P Y Z
J C Q G K P K N I V E S O G E
T P X X R M U C Q W J U N R R
B O W L O A D C H E V N G I D
X H U U F T C A U M V E E L V
S P O O N S N S B U I R D L I
```

KETTLE	OVEN
TO EAT	JUG
FOOD	CHOPSTICKS
FREEZER	GRILL
SPOONS	RECIPE
LADLE	REFRIGERATOR
KNIVES	NAPKIN
APRON	CUPS
SPICES	BOWL
SPONGE	FORKS

32 - Moda

```
X Y K S O E M M O D E R N B P
Q X I T R M I G I R B H X O A
Y N H N I B N I E R V B N U T
L A C E G R I I X A C D B T T
P B I M I O M E P S K C S I E
R U R E N I A G E E I P Q Q R
A T B R A D L J N N B M I U N
C T A U L E I C S U U F P E D
T O F S E R S L I H C D X L N
I N Z A L Y T O V G U I O Y E
C S F E E O S T E U A P L T R
A G I M G V E H F G U S Z S T
L X R O A D D I T E X T U R E
Y J P A N S O N W K V J L D F
D I B O T X M G L C M S M J J
```

EMBROIDERY
BUTTONS
BOUTIQUE
EXPENSIVE
ELEGANT
LACE
STYLE
MEASUREMENTS
MINIMALIST
MODERN

MODEST
ORIGINAL
PATTERN
PRACTICAL
CLOTHING
SIMPLE
FABRIC
TREND
TEXTURE

33 - Electricidad

```
T  K  R  O  W  T  E  N  W  D  V  N  Q  G  E
E  E  V  I  T  A  G  E  N  Y  Q  V  U  E  Q
N  L  L  J  L  R  A  G  Z  G  O  R  A  N  U
G  C  E  E  Q  C  R  E  S  A  L  N  N  E  I
A  V  A  C  V  V  O  D  X  S  U  H  T  R  P
M  P  T  B  T  I  T  S  M  R  G  B  I  A  M
B  U  L  B  L  R  S  E  R  I  W  A  T  T  E
S  B  L  N  Y  E  I  I  K  J  O  T  Y  O  N
T  C  K  T  T  E  C  O  S  T  T  N  R  T
C  P  O  S  I  T  I  V  E  N  P  E  W  N  Y
E  L  E  C  T  R  I  C  I  A  N  R  R  H  F
J  T  L  A  O  X  U  T  K  W  V  Y  U  M  Y
B  K  A  T  E  L  E  P  H  O  N  E  S  X  L
O  X  M  E  D  V  Q  O  C  T  L  L  E  P  J
T  B  P  I  G  U  H  N  A  U  P  O  J  O  K
```

STORAGE	GENERATOR
BATTERY	MAGNET
BULB	LAMP
CABLE	LASER
WIRES	NEGATIVE
QUANTITY	OBJECTS
ELECTRICIAN	POSITIVE
ELECTRIC	NETWORK
SOCKET	TELEVISION
EQUIPMENT	TELEPHONE

34 - Salud y Bienestar #1

```
H  K  G  Q  Q  S  S  T  G  I  J  J  Z  I  H
L  O  H  D  Z  K  V  P  H  R  S  V  Z  B  Y
Z  Z  R  U  D  I  K  Y  I  E  V  I  T  C  A
O  C  J  M  N  N  T  S  M  R  R  P  K  U  H
F  R  K  X  O  G  J  S  E  U  P  A  O  S  E
I  M  F  S  F  N  E  S  D  T  H  P  P  Y  I
D  O  C  T  O  R  E  R  I  C  A  O  V  Y  G
G  L  I  Z  R  I  R  S  C  A  R  S  I  J  H
J  P  N  B  E  O  F  H  I  R  M  T  R  W  T
D  C  I  O  F  Y  E  A  N  F  A  U  U  X  W
H  W  L  N  L  J  W  O  E  J  C  R  S  Q  T
A  D  C  E  E  V  E  P  B  N  Y  E  U  U  N
B  J  T  S  X  R  E  L  A  X  A  T  I  O  N
I  T  R  E  A  T  M  E  N  T  K  S  W  H  N
T  S  H  B  M  U  S  C  L  E  S  Y  Y  E  H
```

ACTIVE
HEIGHT
CLINIC
DOCTOR
PHARMACY
FRACTURE
HUNGER
HABIT
HORMONES
BONES

MEDICINE
MUSCLES
SKIN
POSTURE
REFLEX
RELAXATION
THERAPY
TREATMENT
VIRUS

35 - Adjetivos #2

```
T C Y K E V I T C U D O R P D
I G R F R E S H O N X U E C E
R Y G E W R Y T L A S T S T S
E S R L A M R O N T W Z P G C
D S H S C T I Z O U H J O R R
D E X M I Q I Q S R V J N R I
B M V X T M S V H A J G S P P
P Y A S A O A E E L V I I Y T
Y K T X M E D I B L E S B F I
M H K Z A P R O U D C T L B V
I N T E R E S T I N G R E Y E
E X R L D F A M O U S O F F Q
E L E G A N T D M C N N D Z B
S P I C Y E B C R T E G Y I E
S N Q U X G H G V Y W U A Z J
```

TIRED
EDIBLE
CREATIVE
DESCRIPTIVE
DRAMATIC
ELEGANT
FAMOUS
FRESH
STRONG
INTERESTING

NATURAL
NORMAL
NEW
PROUD
SPICY
PRODUCTIVE
RESPONSIBLE
SALTY
HEALTHY
DRY

36 - Cuerpo Humano

```
Z  W  O  U  Q  L  N  R  Z  Y  F  J  E  L  W
T  O  N  G  U  E  N  B  R  A  I  N  Y  S  O
S  B  J  S  E  J  E  E  C  A  F  J  E  V  Q
P  L  Q  K  K  L  B  O  C  O  A  T  S  W  N
R  E  G  N  I  F  B  T  X  K  N  Y  O  C  A
S  H  O  U  L  D  E  R  A  E  L  K  N  A  H
H  T  U  M  V  O  L  A  H  D  G  K  N  E  E
E  U  H  A  L  O  S  E  D  A  S  K  I  N  Q
A  O  B  K  C  L  I  H  I  J  N  Z  R  Q  H
D  M  S  F  D  B  G  L  R  M  H  D  X  E  J
C  B  R  I  S  C  W  M  O  H  W  L  K  D  E
Z  T  S  Y  S  Z  C  H  I  N  W  A  T  J  V
O  O  V  K  X  V  M  Q  Q  C  O  J  Z  V  E
N  H  J  K  L  C  U  S  O  S  G  R  F  E  L
O  H  C  X  R  F  Q  V  I  O  H  N  F  U  U
```

CHIN	TONGUE
MOUTH	HAND
HEAD	NOSE
FACE	EYE
BRAIN	EAR
ELBOW	SKIN
HEART	LEG
NECK	KNEE
FINGER	BLOOD
SHOULDER	ANKLE

37 - Calentamiento Global

```
G  A  W  D  P  X  Z  U  Q  P  G  F  A  B  P
Z  A  R  A  E  A  C  B  D  V  H  U  T  S  O
M  S  S  C  Z  V  Z  J  L  X  F  T  T  C  P
E  C  R  R  T  J  E  S  A  Z  M  U  E  I  U
K  K  S  K  O  I  H  L  N  Z  M  R  N  E  L
C  R  I  S  I  S  C  W  O  N  B  E  T  N  A
M  L  W  I  W  O  X  J  I  P  X  R  I  T  T
A  P  K  D  Q  E  H  W  T  M  M  H  O  I  I
X  C  L  I  M  A  T  E  A  X  W  E  N  S  O
C  O  N  S  E  Q  U  E  N  C  E  S  N  T  N
D  A  T  A  A  Y  Y  G  R  E  N  E  M  T  S
I  N  D  U  S  T  R  Y  E  W  W  C  X  A  P
D  F  T  M  S  N  O  I  T  A  R  E  N  E  G
V  X  L  A  T  N  E  M  N  O  R  I  V  N  E
B  N  O  I  T  A  L  S  I  G  E  L  R  G  O
```

NOW	DEVELOPMENT
ENVIRONMENTAL	ENERGY
ATTENTION	FUTURE
ARCTIC	GAS
SCIENTIST	GENERATIONS
CLIMATE	INDUSTRY
CONSEQUENCES	INTERNATIONAL
CRISIS	LEGISLATION
DATA	POPULATIONS

38 - Ciencia

```
H Y P O T H E S I S Q Q L M I
E X P E R I M E N T K W A O V
X O M S C I S Y H P O O B L M
R G Y L S L N A T U R E O E C
O R G A N I S M C C F G R C S
D Z K R U S S A T E A W A U K
Y V Y E X S E N Z V M F T L L
K W T N T O L Z J O S D O E W
O N I I D F C H C L K R R S M
H D V M Q D I X L U C J Y U M
A O A W K V T S I T N E I C S
T H R T V B R Y M I X R B Z R
O T G Q A L A Z A O U G J A E
M E C T T G P S T N A L P Y T
W M Z L A C I M E H C D U L L
```

ATOM	HYPOTHESIS
SCIENTIST	LABORATORY
CLIMATE	METHOD
DATA	MINERALS
EVOLUTION	MOLECULES
EXPERIMENT	NATURE
PHYSICS	ORGANISM
FOSSIL	PARTICLES
GRAVITY	PLANTS
FACT	CHEMICAL

39 - Restaurante #2

```
V  E  G  E  T  A  B  L  E  S  E  L  D  M  D
J  F  L  D  S  T  Y  H  H  F  S  L  D  B  O
K  P  L  R  I  A  H  C  L  G  D  G  Z  E  V
H  T  Q  Z  K  N  I  T  H  T  N  Q  J  S  J
C  L  M  A  M  T  N  S  G  G  E  N  Z  F  J
N  A  Y  V  G  V  P  E  G  A  R  E  V  E  B
U  S  K  B  D  J  B  C  R  E  T  I  A  W  Z
L  O  B  E  I  C  E  I  A  E  V  P  K  K  E
M  U  Y  J  Z  W  F  P  I  N  T  I  U  R  F
W  P  K  A  L  H  B  S  I  O  S  A  L  A  D
M  B  E  D  E  L  I  C  I  O  U  S  W  S  I
K  D  X  B  R  L  T  J  U  P  S  F  S  J  P
B  S  Q  N  H  A  X  F  I  S  H  O  Z  T  W
I  A  P  P  E  T  I  Z  E  R  O  R  T  I  A
F  X  U  P  L  I  J  L  A  S  Q  K  M  X  H
```

WATER	FRUIT
LUNCH	ICE
APPETIZER	EGGS
BEVERAGE	CAKE
WAITER	FISH
DINNER	SALT
SPOON	CHAIR
DELICIOUS	SOUP
SALAD	FORK
SPICES	VEGETABLES

40 - Profesiones #1

```
J V M Z L C G S B D S V B C A
R E M O N O R T S A H C A O C
E T W A O Z B J P C H W N Z E
C E E E O S A P Y I R H K O D
N L R O L N I D L I A Q E E I
A H J B F E P W U U R N R E T
D T N D A O R Z N J M M I Y O
H A A T T O R N E Y G B U S R
A M B A S S A D O R R I E R T
F I R E F I G H T E R I S R L
X I G E O L O G I S T X R H U
C A R T O G R A P H E R U T Q
P S Y C H O L O G I S T N A O
A R H U N T E R D O C T O R A
M U S I C I A N I E I A I X F
```

ATTORNEY   AMBASSADOR
ASTRONOMER   NURSE
ATHLETE   COACH
DANCER   PLUMBER
BANKER   GEOLOGIST
FIREFIGHTER   JEWELER
CARTOGRAPHER   MUSICIAN
HUNTER   PIANIST
DOCTOR   PSYCHOLOGIST
EDITOR

41 - Geometría

```
D C A L C U L A T I O N X R D
T I W Z L A C I T R E V I W I
N E M Z A Y M Z F B B M E G A
C N L E T N E M G E S F V X M
U Q I L N O I T R O P O R P E
N G U G O S B R A V J D U Y T
E W L N Z S I K Y I C H C R E
L G S A I A X O H E I G H T R
G M Z I R M X L N M O I Q E N
N C H R O N O I T A U Q E M X
A U N T H J V F L D I W W M Y
Q Z M S U R F A C E R D S Y U
B R E B T H E O R Y C M E S C
S S S L E L L A R A P C Z M O
I E Q R I R V W T W L O G I C
```

HEIGHT   MEDIAN
ANGLE   NUMBER
CALCULATION   PARALLEL
CURVE   PROPORTION
DIAMETER   SEGMENT
DIMENSION   SYMMETRY
EQUATION   SURFACE
HORIZONTAL   THEORY
LOGIC   TRIANGLE
MASS   VERTICAL

42 - Baile

```
G  L  P  V  D  Y  G  S  Y  J  G  J  M  L  X
T  C  M  U  Z  L  C  K  X  C  N  Y  U  Z  M
Z  N  N  O  T  N  E  M  E  V  O  M  C  M  E
R  E  N  T  R  A  P  T  C  N  C  E  B  K  P
P  E  R  U  T  L  U  C  I  O  Y  D  O  B  T
O  V  H  D  C  L  A  S  S  I  C  A  L  B  R
S  I  G  E  C  A  R  G  U  T  F  C  A  J  A
T  S  C  L  A  X  G  L  M  O  R  A  R  K  D
U  S  V  K  C  R  O  B  X  M  P  A  U  O  I
R  E  U  K  L  I  S  F  U  E  M  U  T  J  T
E  R  U  S  U  X  E  A  S  B  W  Z  L  P  I
K  P  M  C  F  O  I  D  L  J  X  I  U  C  O
R  X  R  H  Y  T  H  M  C  A  E  N  C  V  N
O  E  L  J  O  V  I  S  U  A  L  Y  K  D  A
B  O  S  G  J  C  J  S  R  G  G  S  N  F  L
```

ACADEMY	GRACE
JOYFUL	MOVEMENT
ART	MUSIC
CLASSICAL	POSTURE
BODY	RHYTHM
CULTURE	JUMP
CULTURAL	PARTNER
EMOTION	TRADITIONAL
REHEARSAL	VISUAL
EXPRESSIVE	

43 - Matemáticas

```
S F H Q Y N W Y X A N G L E S
Y R E T E M A I D E X S H Z Q
M A M S E X P O N E N T Z J S
M C Y A V O L U M E U X B P M
E T X D R Z C N M B I P M X G
T I I W Z G E N O I T A U Q E
R O K Q F N O G Y L O P W X O
Y N D X P X S L A M I C E D M
P A R A L L E L E R E H P S E
I H E T R I A N G L E R I C T
R E C T A N G L E X L O T Q R
R A D I U S U Z B E Y A L R Y
P E R I M E T E R O T T R E E
P E R P E N D I C U L A R A E
A R I T H M E T I C I A Z H P
```

ARITHMETIC	PARALLELOGRAM
ANGLES	PERIMETER
DECIMAL	PERPENDICULAR
DIAMETER	POLYGON
EQUATION	RADIUS
SPHERE	RECTANGLE
EXPONENT	SYMMETRY
FRACTION	TRIANGLE
GEOMETRY	VOLUME
PARALLEL	

44 - Restaurante #1

```
B F M J D X K G N E H C T I K
O H M E D Z O B N L W H S N R
W R N D A H O J O L K I A G P
L K Q X A T Y C I P S C U R Y
C O F F E E G Y T W D K C E X
C A S H I E R X A M P E E D Q
C U W G Z C E B V G E N J I E
J R M Q B O L N R D F N A E T
O E D T T C L F E E I I U N D
P L A T E W A O S S N K R T T
V A L A M G Y O E S K P P S S
I J U E Q Y K D R E T A D T S
D S S O K P C Y M R I N Q N M
U R B T I C E M N T E Y X U C
E G I W A I T R E S S M S J D
```

ALLERGY
COFFEE
CASHIER
WAITRESS
MEAT
KITCHEN
TO EAT
FOOD
KNIFE
INGREDIENTS

MENU
BREAD
SPICY
PLATE
CHICKEN
DESSERT
RESERVATION
SAUCE
NAPKIN
BOWL

45 - Profesiones #2

```
C  H  O  H  J  E  N  G  I  N  E  E  R  A  A
N  M  J  X  R  O  T  A  R  T  S  U  L  L  I
O  K  I  X  E  T  U  A  N  O  R  T  S  A  B
Q  L  L  S  H  W  E  R  F  W  M  O  B  Q  I
Q  D  V  B  P  V  V  H  N  E  E  L  D  D  O
L  I  B  R  A  R  I  A  N  A  Z  I  Z  Y  L
T  T  B  E  R  E  T  R  A  S  L  P  U  S  O
E  E  R  N  G  T  C  A  I  U  T  I  T  B  G
Q  A  O  E  O  N  E  P  C  R  D  J  S  C  I
O  C  T  D  T  I  T  O  I  G  W  M  I  T  S
P  H  N  R  O  A  E  M  S  E  I  W  T  T  T
T  E  E  A  H  P  D  S  Y  O  W  I  N  G  R
V  R  V  G  P  G  P  J  H  N  Q  E  E  O  F
L  I  N  G  U  I  S  T  P  Q  X  X  D  O  M
P  H  I  L  O  S  O  P  H  E  R  F  H  E  G
```

ASTRONAUT
LIBRARIAN
BIOLOGIST
SURGEON
DENTIST
DETECTIVE
PHILOSOPHER
PHOTOGRAPHER
ILLUSTRATOR

ENGINEER
INVENTOR
GARDENER
LINGUIST
PHYSICIAN
JOURNALIST
PILOT
PAINTER
TEACHER

46 - Senderismo

```
E M P O T G L V Z Z U Q S P N
M O M R I V U N O K A D T R M
J S E I R F F I L C O N O E Y
X Q C E E C P X D L I W N P G
K U I N D M S V F E K Y E A T
P I X T M J S O M R S P S R O
A T P A M O P T K U K D L A I
E O H T Z M U B H T R Y A T V
T E S I L E K N A A A Y M I H
K S T O O B A M T N P T I O J
K W E N W T W Z R A I J N N C
O F A H E A V Y J G I N A F O
S C P T I M M U S Q Z N C V Q
U E B P E T A M I L C V I C S
N U L C D R C A M P I N G F R
```

CLIFF   MOUNTAIN
WATER   MOSQUITOES
ANIMALS   NATURE
BOOTS   ORIENTATION
CAMPING   PARKS
TIRED   HEAVY
CLIMATE   STONES
SUMMIT   PREPARATION
GUIDES   WILD
MAP   SUN

47 - Naturaleza

```
O A P J S E E B O R G A T A G
Q N M Z U H Q Y D F F N R R L
R I V E R X E N E R E S O C A
U I G R L K D L I W X D P T C
F T O V L P W P T W Q U I I I
R Y F O R E S T E E W O C C E
E R O S I O N D A A R L A W R
B A D E S E R T Y O C C L D Z
E U A N I M A L S N Z E V X C
A T F O L I A G E V A N F G N
U C X L F X E A C I Z M Z U S
T N M X T I S G W T F E I Q L
Y A H M D W M U M A Q G X C R
Q S E S H L M E U L W D O Q V
S X T F P B V G Y M D Z D Q Z
```

BEES
ANIMALS
ARCTIC
BEAUTY
FOREST
DESERT
DYNAMIC
EROSION
FOLIAGE
GLACIER

FOG
CLOUDS
PEACEFUL
SHELTER
RIVER
WILD
SANCTUARY
SERENE
TROPICAL
VITAL

48 - Conduciendo

```
B F O I G L L M P R F Y P M S
X R D A N G E R O Y L K E O P
L A A O I S R O P T I E D T E
S C E K C U R T F E O H E O E
U I G T E E R T S F Y R S R D
H F G N Z S E M A A Q C T C N
I F E E I W X B G S R I R Y J
F A T D S O D U W B J V I C U
O R H I L I C E N S E B A L M
G T X C E O D J Q P C U N E T
U A N C U Q F M A P I S R A Q
H P R A F W B W F E L N I T R
D E W A M B K T K N O D V Q I
I X D Q G W K L X U P J K L U
P C A X L E N N U T R Q T W C
```

ACCIDENT
BUS
STREET
TRUCK
CAR
FUEL
BRAKES
GARAGE
GAS
LICENSE

MAP
MOTORCYCLE
MOTOR
PEDESTRIAN
DANGER
POLICE
SAFETY
TRAFFIC
TUNNEL
SPEED

49 - Ballet

```
A J K K P J O S Y E R E R D C
R K U O O L R K K V W C E A H
T I P W C R C E E I C G H N O
I G B Z C J H B Y S L X E C R
S I X I O I E W M S F L A E E
T B S I G Z S U U E C A R R O
I E L E C I T C A R P U S S G
C S T Y L E R C J P R D A N R
L U W Y T C A Z T X H I L B A
E A E R U T S E G E Y E R N P
S L S B H Y P U D X T N O M H
S P W D R J H S M N H C Z U Y
O P U G S V D Z X A M E J S V
N A N I R E L L A B M O W I M
S W J R L C O M P O S E R C T
```

APPLAUSE   EXPRESSIVE
ARTISTIC   GESTURE
AUDIENCE   SKILL
BALLERINA   LESSONS
DANCERS   MUSCLES
COMPOSER   MUSIC
CHOREOGRAPHY   ORCHESTRA
REHEARSAL   PRACTICE
STYLE   RHYTHM

50 - Fuerza y Gravedad

```
D  I  S  C  O  V  E  R  Y  H  M  T  J  P  H
G  L  R  T  L  K  G  G  P  V  A  P  F  L  X
M  E  C  H  A  N  I  C  S  I  G  H  A  A  A
S  D  I  G  S  K  A  G  I  S  N  Y  R  N  J
U  U  M  I  R  M  Y  D  X  E  E  S  S  E  E
Z  T  A  E  E  H  T  G  A  I  T  I  S  T  X
J  I  N  W  V  L  I  I  E  T  I  C  N  S  P
N  N  Y  G  I  M  B  J  M  R  S  S  Q  H  A
B  G  D  T  N  S  R  S  K  E  M  E  T  E  N
I  A  E  O  U  O  O  A  S  P  V  V  L  B  S
B  M  E  F  R  I  C  T  I  O  N  E  D  H  I
Y  F  P  C  E  N  T  E  R  R  A  T  V  L  O
G  F  S  A  G  N  V  Y  R  P  V  Q  D  X  N
S  E  P  J  C  P  R  E  S  S  U  R  E  Q  D
L  S  D  D  L  T  D  I  S  T  A  N  C  E  O
```

CENTER	MAGNITUDE
DISCOVERY	MECHANICS
DYNAMIC	ORBIT
DISTANCE	WEIGHT
AXIS	PLANETS
EXPANSION	PRESSURE
PHYSICS	PROPERTIES
FRICTION	TIME
IMPACT	UNIVERSAL
MAGNETISM	SPEED

51 - Aventura

```
P H D A S E L I V W H V S N J
R S A N O N A V I G A T I O N
E Z N E X O U Y W N N I C I O
P R G W I G S T Y I A T H S I
A N E B E A U T Y S T I A R T
R F R Z Q B N H T I U N N U A
A R O Z C T U V E R R E C C N
T I U J Q F T I F P E R E X I
I E S C S L E V A R T A P E T
O N W X K J N O S U H R C Y S
N D J T I S Y V E S T Y Y M E
U S R O D I F F I C U L T Y D
T G R W Y T I V I T C A Y J S
B R A V E R Y T I B I Q I I I
E N T H U S I A S M D O L Z L
```

ACTIVITY	NATURE
JOY	NAVIGATION
FRIENDS	NEW
BEAUTY	CHANCE
DESTINATION	DANGEROUS
DIFFICULTY	PREPARATION
ENTHUSIASM	SAFETY
EXCURSION	SURPRISING
UNUSUAL	BRAVERY
ITINERARY	TRAVELS

52 - Pájaros

```
A N Z J Z Z C U L W N N J Y E
L U H C O I A E L G A E I M G
F I E O S J S S G X C K J F P
D U C K Z T D O O G I C C O G
N W Y M D K R O T S L I L H X
U N L U L W L G R K E H Z I H
O I W H N A C U O T P C J W R
G U L L S H A D Y Y G O O Q R
N G W N H V F R O G P V T V B
I N O O K C U C Q F A M K X G
M E R L Y T I L T X R S P H O
A P R M J Z L R E D R C W Q S
L W A H E R O N T L O D O A W
F E P S B N C V B S T X R Y N
S W S Q O D P I G E O N C H G
```

OSTRICH	SPARROW
EAGLE	HAWK
STORK	EGG
SWAN	PARROT
CUCKOO	PIGEON
CROW	DUCK
FLAMINGO	PELICAN
GOOSE	PENGUIN
HERON	CHICKEN
GULL	TOUCAN

53 - Geografía

```
W O R L D M D P P E E A R F L
N L I E I K H Q Q K P T E F X
L A U D V K R H Z X S L N R Q
O T J U K I X O N O K A M A P
N I J T A P R X A L G S J O W
G T L I E R E H P S I M E H E
I U W T L U P H P N O H H C S
T D M L X W O N H C O U C M T
U E E A C R E G I O N R T H U
D I R E D K F A D A R J T H H
E S I S C O N T I N E N T H A
X L D T E R R I T O R Y H H I
K A I O S C O U N T R Y T I C
S N A I H H T C M G W G W T H
H D N I A T N U O M S B T V N
```

ALTITUDE

ATLAS

CITY

CONTINENT

HEMISPHERE

ISLAND

LATITUDE

LONGITUDE

MAP

SEA

MERIDIAN

MOUNTAIN

WORLD

NORTH

WEST

COUNTRY

REGION

RIVER

SOUTH

TERRITORY

54 - Música

```
M L H V B T B J E R N X P M H
H E F O D E A R E P O X D I A
T G L Y V M L H Z N K V D C R
Y I O O U P L I X P P B T R M
H W X Y D O A O U J A E A O O
R H R N J Y D T Q X X E L P N
S I N G E R C H O R U S B H I
C L A S S I C A L D A Y U O C
G I W R E C O R D I N G M N H
J R T M U S I C A L E N Z E A
U C W E V O C A L Q Z I A M R
I M P R O V I S E H H S J I M
K P V H Q P M U S I C I A N O
I N S T R U M E N T V T C D N
W C C D G J M V U A M L R W Y
```

HARMONY	INSTRUMENT
HARMONIC	MELODY
ALBUM	MICROPHONE
BALLAD	MUSICAL
SINGER	MUSICIAN
SING	OPERA
CLASSICAL	POETIC
CHORUS	RHYTHM
RECORDING	TEMPO
IMPROVISE	VOCAL

55 - Enfermedad

```
C C O D N P U L M O N A R Y I
G O H S S E I G R E L L A X A
E X N R S O U W E L L N E S S
N A O T O P A R H E A L T H F
E P Y R A N Y O O O Y M X L A
T I F A A G I D I P R N Z A L
I M S E B V I C O G A U Q P U
C M Y H D W G O R C T T A A M
A U N J O I C H U X I W H I B
M N D C M B O D Y S D X M Y A
D I R G I W E A K E E F P Y R
M T O L N G P C K N R W M H R
O Y M F A Z L Q R O E M G L U
N Q E P L M V Y Y B H X Q O K
I N F L A M M A T I O N W I E
```

ABDOMINAL
ALLERGIES
WELLNESS
CONTAGIOUS
HEART
CHRONIC
BODY
WEAK
GENETIC

HEREDITARY
BONES
INFLAMMATION
IMMUNITY
LUMBAR
NEUROPATHY
PULMONARY
HEALTH
SYNDROME

56 - Actividades

```
H G O X F W Z L L L I K S K P
B A N A I Q C S E L Z Z U P H
T Y P R S I G N I H S I F D O
P H H D B K Q K S G Z P V J T
A C T I V I T Y U E A H B H O
H P C R R R D M R S W M S O G
I U B E R U S A E L P N E D R
N C X L U N H C M A G I C S A
T Z B A F J P A I N T I N G P
E N F X R U T C U M R N B P H
R W N A C R A F T S A A R M Y
E J I T S E W I N G N R U Q S
S G N I D A E R E I Y J E N K
T I S O G A R D E N I N G C K
S U G N I T N U H H I K I N G
```

ACTIVITY	GAMES
ART	READING
CRAFTS	MAGIC
HUNTING	LEISURE
CERAMICS	FISHING
SEWING	PAINTING
PHOTOGRAPHY	PLEASURE
SKILL	RELAXATION
INTERESTS	PUZZLES
GARDENING	HIKING

57 - Instrumentos Musicales

```
C S D T I L Q D O E M B X G N
T L I R B Y G E P H A X A N B
R S A B M I R A M S N L V J Z
O A W R A T I U G M D P Q Z M
M X M Z I G R M M Z O N A I P
B O S G P N G A T A L U A M R
O P H A S O E O B O I P V P A
N H A W A G E T T G N Z O O H
E O R V I O L I N R F L U T E
S N M J W N O I S S U C R E P
M E O L L E C C N M D M N Y N
E E N I R U O B M A T R P U S
G U I B A S S O O N D C U E E
D B C B A N J O Q S X L S M T
C Z A F Q A E D U B I D P Y E
```

HARMONICA
HARP
BANJO
CLARINET
BASSOON
FLUTE
GONG
GUITAR
MANDOLIN
MARIMBA

OBOE
TAMBOURINE
PERCUSSION
PIANO
SAXOPHONE
DRUM
TROMBONE
TRUMPET
VIOLIN
CELLO

58 - Formas

```
W D A C X P C C Q P L L Z S W
A I L O R O Y I P R E J M F U
P B O N M L L R B R W A N O J
M Y B E A Y I C I T S J P L D
F R R T G G N L A R E N R O C
S O E A Z O D E R B G M I K A
S H P Y M N E L A E D I S N J
C P Y N N I R E P Q E I M J D
C U H H Q O D A R C C V Y S W
U S C E R A U Q S U W Y R I A
B D K E R O B L I N E B P U B
E U A R B E C O E D P H T N C
E L L I P S E V R S S N O M N
M R H E L G N A I R T D O U C
Y L I U R H E L G N A T C E R
```

ARC	CORNER
EDGES	HYPERBOLA
CYLINDER	SIDE
CIRCLE	LINE
CONE	OVAL
SQUARE	PYRAMID
CUBE	POLYGON
CURVE	PRISM
ELLIPSE	RECTANGLE
SPHERE	TRIANGLE

59 - Flores

```
V I H B G I T H M T A H P W R
E N I M S A J W Q Y N F E Y O
Y Y B M W O R E V O L C O T C
A P I L U T E D T F R R N A L
J F S T K O D I E Q N O Y T O
S C C I L S N H U N D S S K N
Z B U X N S E C Q O I E I A M
O L S A W R V R U I P A A F W
C A K L W T A O O L X E D G S
X S R J I B L I B E L N T W D
L I L A C L W L I D O F F A D
P O P P Y X Y U Q N N Q V V L
S U N F L O W E R A V S H W M
C A L E N D U L A D C K K J I
Z K M A G N O L I A T U Z P M
```

POPPY

CALENDULA

DANDELION

GARDENIA

SUNFLOWER

HIBISCUS

JASMINE

LAVENDER

LILAC

LILY

MAGNOLIA

DAISY

DAFFODIL

ORCHID

PEONY

PETAL

BOUQUET

ROSE

CLOVER

TULIP

60 - Astronomía

```
E S A C A X Y J Y O I U R M C
M A M Y K S V B F W P H O O O
E L R W U E T E N A L P C O N
T Q J T D I O R E T S A K N S
E P I D H Z M N O O Y H E A T
O V A V Z T O A S N R C T O E
R T P S U H T V G E O J A O L
R A D I A T I O N Q T M X M L
A X K E P T H N C U A A E W A
P E A M J O A R O I V Q S R T
D R M V F C V E S N R H K T I
G A L A X Y Y P M O E M Y A O
C K V Y T Q D U O X S H N I N
E C L I P S E S S S B D M C C
A S T R O N A U T U O B N E F
```

ASTEROID	GALAXY
ASTRONAUT	MOON
ASTRONOMER	METEOR
SKY	OBSERVATORY
ROCKET	PLANET
CONSTELLATION	RADIATION
COSMOS	SUPERNOVA
ECLIPSE	EARTH
EQUINOX	

61 - Paisajes

```
R  I  V  E  R  T  Y  J  J  L  D  D  Y  X  H
D  D  R  O  W  E  I  H  B  C  O  N  X  Z  N
I  D  A  B  J  I  U  P  G  V  N  M  W  S  V
M  C  L  A  K  E  V  A  C  D  A  S  D  L  U
O  R  E  S  Y  E  G  Z  R  N  C  T  Q  D  V
U  D  X  B  F  N  O  O  G  A  L  U  W  L  D
N  N  S  K  E  D  H  A  G  L  O  N  N  L  S
T  L  N  V  I  R  F  S  S  S  V  D  B  A  B
A  E  Z  G  C  X  G  W  L  I  Z  R  R  F  U
I  S  Y  X  N  H  C  A  E  B  S  A  A  R  H
N  T  R  E  S  E  D  M  Z  V  A  L  L  E  Y
T  U  P  C  L  O  B  P  I  S  Q  R  H  T  I
J  A  L  U  S  N  I  N  E  P  S  W  O  A  V
T  R  E  I  C  A  L  G  F  G  H  B  S  W  B
N  Y  F  S  L  Y  J  R  T  N  V  L  E  W  Y
```

WATERFALL	SEA
CAVE	MOUNTAIN
DESERT	OASIS
ESTUARY	SWAMP
GEYSER	PENINSULA
GLACIER	BEACH
ICEBERG	RIVER
ISLAND	TUNDRA
LAKE	VALLEY
LAGOON	VOLCANO

62 - Días y Meses

```
M S A Q C H Q W T V D K A A F
Y A D S E U T K N W R H P U R
H T N O M H U T Y T C A R G I
M U J A N U A R Y I H X I U D
U R A E Y R A U R B E F L S A
H D H I N W O C T O B E R T Y
Y A D S R U H T Q S U N E B W
A Y N T C V J X P R B A X Q E
D A D Y A S E P T E M B E R E
S D F Q L M O N D A Y L U J K
E N P S E N T J S A J T E G Q
N U Y X N G B A M V M T J F F
D S P Z D Y I I D O T A S C P
E H G G A H O G J D A F P P N
W K W E R E B M E V O N F B X
```

APRIL
AUGUST
YEAR
CALENDAR
SUNDAY
JANUARY
FEBRUARY
THURSDAY
JULY
JUNE

MONDAY
TUESDAY
MONTH
WEDNESDAY
NOVEMBER
OCTOBER
SATURDAY
WEEK
SEPTEMBER
FRIDAY

63 - Biología

```
O  E  K  V  E  N  E  R  V  E  C  C  C  S  D
D  S  O  Y  W  M  V  U  I  N  H  E  O  Y  E
R  T  M  N  F  Z  B  Z  Q  O  R  L  L  M  J
Z  N  I  O  Q  J  V  R  Q  M  O  L  L  B  K
D  A  A  R  S  G  C  T  Y  R  M  B  A  I  F
I  L  O  U  E  I  X  S  C  O  O  A  G  O  P
M  P  F  E  K  N  S  S  L  H  S  C  E  S  S
L  V  L  N  U  X  Z  L  N  A  O  T  N  I  D
A  N  A  T  O  M  Y  Y  N  N  M  E  T  S  N
R  Y  M  J  R  D  U  S  M  I  E  R  A  R  Q
U  M  M  L  E  J  Q  X  Y  E  V  I  S  S  I
T  X  A  Z  X  D  A  R  U  T  T  A  X  G  M
A  U  M  N  O  I  T  U  L  O  V  E  Y  F  V
N  O  I  T  A  T  U  M  M  R  I  X  U  T  V
R  E  P  T  I  L  E  E  S  P  A  N  Y  S  S
```

ANATOMY	MUTATION
BACTERIA	NATURAL
CELL	NERVE
COLLAGEN	NEURON
CHROMOSOME	OSMOSIS
EMBRYO	PLANTS
ENZYME	PROTEIN
EVOLUTION	REPTILE
HORMONE	SYMBIOSIS
MAMMAL	SYNAPSE

64 - Jardinería

```
G U J Z A E L B I D E F S X S
E Y N Z D X T C P A S L P F B
K Y L A N O S A E S O O E S Q
X D N G K T H Z M I H R C Q H
L E A F F I R G Y I A A I S L
I D O Y M C T J U Q L L E V I
O L Y F O L I A G E E C S S L
S E S D S V O S E E D S Y Z A
B O G I S Y R E N I A T N O C
W O M R O H C T W G V S I X I
F A U T L I H J N U F O T W N
X M T Q B W A M U I Y P G O A
P F Y E U L R E N W F M Z E T
L O N Y R E D O D O Y O B Y O
M N T E R U T S I O M C J W B
```

WATER
BOTANICAL
CLIMATE
EDIBLE
COMPOST
CONTAINER
SPECIES
SEASONAL
EXOTIC
BLOSSOM

FLORAL
FOLIAGE
LEAF
ORCHARD
MOISTURE
HOSE
BOUQUET
SEEDS
DIRT
SOIL

65 - Chocolate

```
P  F  L  B  C  A  R  A  M  E  L  E  P  F  P
O  S  Y  I  P  J  E  C  E  X  O  T  I  C  E
W  U  F  T  D  P  R  O  P  I  Q  I  A  I  A
D  G  I  T  I  Z  O  C  I  S  E  R  A  N  N
E  A  A  E  K  L  V  O  C  W  O  O  Q  G  U
R  R  U  R  Z  I  A  N  E  E  Z  V  N  R  T
C  A  C  A  O  O  L  U  R  E  K  A  O  E  S
Y  Q  X  X  Y  E  F  T  Q  T  Z  F  R  D  P
A  R  O  M  A  C  A  L  O  R  I  E  S  I  H
D  E  L  I  C  I  O  U  S  Z  S  Z  P  E  P
V  Z  H  T  A  S  T  E  B  Q  U  P  C  N  H
I  K  Q  K  K  H  B  U  D  P  C  F  P  T  L
X  O  A  Z  K  I  N  U  Z  I  T  G  J  V  J
G  S  H  P  A  N  T  I  O  X  I  D  A  N  T
A  R  T  I  S  A  N  A  L  H  T  A  B  G  D
```

BITTER	COCONUT
ANTIOXIDANT	DELICIOUS
AROMA	SWEET
ARTISANAL	EXOTIC
SUGAR	FAVORITE
PEANUTS	TASTE
CACAO	INGREDIENT
QUALITY	POWDER
CALORIES	RECIPE
CARAMEL	FLAVOR

66 - Barbacoas

```
G  B  B  M  U  W  S  N  H  U  D  B  R  F  S
L  B  Q  O  N  N  Q  W  U  S  A  U  C  E  A
G  R  G  W  L  R  V  N  N  S  M  O  B  Z  L
O  C  H  I  C  K  E  N  G  Q  D  A  U  G  A
N  G  U  J  S  V  E  W  E  R  O  F  U  F  D
I  P  E  P  P  E  R  U  R  E  M  M  U  S  S
O  U  H  U  E  L  F  J  R  N  G  R  I  L  L
N  D  V  Y  F  U  A  M  A  N  T  O  H  G  R
S  E  M  A  G  N  M  C  H  I  L  D  R  E  N
K  M  F  E  Z  C  I  U  Y  D  A  G  Q  T  Z
N  U  J  R  R  H  L  Q  C  L  S  Y  J  C  L
I  S  W  F  U  N  Y  T  O  M  A  T  O  E  S
V  I  F  L  T  I  W  Z  M  L  R  R  F  C  Z
E  C  F  P  A  Z  T  T  S  T  W  N  W  H  F
S  B  V  V  V  E  G  E  T  A  B  L  E  S  C
```

LUNCH	MUSIC
HOT	CHILDREN
ONIONS	GRILL
DINNER	PEPPER
KNIVES	CHICKEN
SALADS	SALT
FAMILY	SAUCE
FRUIT	TOMATOES
HUNGER	SUMMER
GAMES	VEGETABLES

67 - Ropa

```
I S I J P V S B U P M S Q D H
S C R E K P S C R D Z C D J A
B D V N O H H O S T N A P S T
O E N E C K L A C E J R A S R
V S L P A J A M A S Z F P B I
Q U X T F C O A T E T Y R K H
D O O E T A C D Y X I Q O R S
P L S L C S S E V O L G N D E
S B H E M V V H J E W E L R Y
A W O C H H L O I J C H L Y Y
N K E A D E T G S O A S X K I
D N T R E T A E W S N C C Q K
A A L B A K S O S W T N K P P
L S K I R T T J E Y T A R E U
S S E R D I E S F A K N I N T
```

COAT

BLOUSE

SCARF

SHIRT

JACKET

BELT

NECKLACE

APRON

SKIRT

GLOVES

JEWELRY

FASHION

PANTS

PAJAMAS

BRACELET

SANDALS

HAT

SWEATER

DRESS

SHOE

68 - Meditación

```
K  L  A  T  N  E  M  F  U  F  Q  A  D  B  X
I  D  E  T  N  E  M  E  V  O  M  C  N  R  C
N  E  D  U  T  I  T  A  R  G  L  C  K  V  Z
D  M  N  I  G  E  X  S  S  G  A  E  G  C  L
N  Y  I  W  R  U  N  M  G  T  C  P  A  L  T
E  N  M  B  U  A  A  T  F  P  L  T  X  Z  Z
S  F  B  M  C  E  G  N  I  H  T  A  E  R  B
S  C  L  A  R  I  T  Y  P  O  E  N  E  J  Z
C  O  M  P  A  S  S  I  O  N  N  C  C  T  G
X  M  N  A  T  U  R  E  I  T  Y  E  A  W  Y
J  U  O  B  S  E  R  V  A  T  I  O  N  E  F
I  S  N  O  I  T  O  M  E  R  U  T  S  O  P
A  I  L  N  K  L  G  T  H  O  U  G  H  T  S
G  C  P  E  R  S  P  E  C  T  I  V  E  X  D
S  I  L  E  N  C  E  B  Z  S  K  V  D  G  M
```

ACCEPTANCE
ATTENTION
KINDNESS
CALM
CLARITY
COMPASSION
EMOTIONS
GRATITUDE
MENTAL
MIND

MOVEMENT
MUSIC
NATURE
OBSERVATION
PEACE
THOUGHTS
PERSPECTIVE
POSTURE
BREATHING
SILENCE

69 - Café

```
Y B D T U E S Y F R Y X J E Y
R J I L D V H C F I K X B L M
U J U T B O A F D I L Y Z B B
G G Q H T O E C Y F I T W N L
C O I C G E U Y B X M Z E Q A
C J L C C T R C Z K A H C R C
M O R N I N G S U J E B I O K
C I D I C A H U B Q R P R V I
G A G R I N D W O Y C G P A R
X U F Q P I T A M O R A N L P
G E Q F X S X T U H T A Z F X
P S Z N E V D E T S A O R D G
X L Y F U I Y R A G U S O D N
T S I N U I N I G I R O C U P
V A R I E T Y E G A R E V E B
```

WATER	MILK
BITTER	LIQUID
AROMA	MORNING
ROASTED	GRIND
SUGAR	BLACK
ACIDIC	ORIGIN
BEVERAGE	PRICE
CAFFEINE	FLAVOR
CREAM	CUP
FILTER	VARIETY

70 - Libros

```
E A R W C T R A G I C E G H J
S T O R Y O G D P G T C U T F
U B H O R R N E T T I R W G A
O Q T T A J P T V X R F C N F
R O U A R E D A E R J M Y O W
O L A R E Q U J G X Z O Z I S
M O Y R T E O P A D T E T T M
U K W A I Q A Y P G W M E C N
H P L N L I N V E N T I V E O
B G O Y H I S T O R I C A L V
E V F E X D Q E W L N K Z L E
B O L R M P W J I P C G T O L
D U A L I T Y K W R O X R C M
A D V E N T U R E C E S X D N
R E L E V A N T G R I S G M J
```

AUTHOR
ADVENTURE
COLLECTION
CONTEXT
DUALITY
WRITTEN
STORY
HISTORICAL
HUMOROUS
INVENTIVE

READER
LITERARY
NARRATOR
NOVEL
PAGE
RELEVANT
POEM
POETRY
SERIES
TRAGIC

71 - Nutrición

```
C C A R B O H Y D R A T E S H
E C U A S F Q D I E T M Y P E
R P R O T E I N S L E B D W A
E F E R M E N T A T I O N E L
A B B A E D I B L E L V O I T
L I R A P Y R H G N W I I G H
S T J Y L P I O C V P T T H Y
E T H T L A E H K M F A S T T
I E R X O U N T I Y R M E N I
R R O V A L F C I Y R I G E L
O V E F K T Y V E T S N I I A
L W B K Q B O W W D E P D R U
A U T E B N B X Z A E M J T Q
C P X G W J J T I Y H H C U A
H Y J U Y A D M I N V N A N Q
```

BITTER
APPETITE
QUALITY
CALORIES
CARBOHYDRATES
CEREALS
EDIBLE
DIET
DIGESTION
BALANCED

FERMENTATION
NUTRIENT
WEIGHT
PROTEINS
FLAVOR
SAUCE
HEALTH
HEALTHY
TOXIN
VITAMIN

72 - Edificios

```
C B M F F M S O X A X E S F M
D M S I K Q X N B M R M C A X
S U P E R M A R K E T B H R U
P I Q G H L K L Z N O A O M X
C D G A O L A T I P S O H H
G A Y R N R T T A C I S L A W
Z T L A F C C E H N A Y N Q E
J S N G Z K X V L E K E L C H
F A C T O R Y L J J A L T E O
L A B O R A T O R Y D T N D S
J Y B Y N J E V Q C O S E O T
O Q A Q P M U S E U M A D R E
B G R E W O T X U O W C F V L
D T N E M T R A P A J D W Z E
D M F O B S E R V A T O R Y H
```

HOSTEL
APARTMENT
CASTLE
CINEMA
EMBASSY
SCHOOL
STADIUM
FACTORY
GARAGE
BARN

FARM
HOSPITAL
HOTEL
LABORATORY
MUSEUM
OBSERVATORY
SUPERMARKET
THEATER
TOWER

73 - Océano

```
S W J N G T L A S Y T H L C U
H H E E O U S C X P M I R H S
A A U H Y N I H P L O D D B L
R L U O S A T C Y S A E Q E Z
K E D Z T I R Q T C E Q A A S
Y E Q K E G F E E R O B I G U
F I Z M R O T S L D J R A L P
H F B P E J K T T J E D A A O
B O A T Y Y X W R V L S F L T
B F C L X K R N U Y L P E O C
E V E R K W O Z T F Y Y E U O
L P X A F P Y U D N F Q L J E
I Y P I T R B P L C I C C M L
S P O N G E A D V H S X S T K
M H G P N A C R A B H M Z D B
```

ALGAE
EEL
REEF
TUNA
WHALE
BOAT
SHRIMP
CRAB
CORAL
DOLPHIN

SPONGE
TIDES
JELLYFISH
OYSTER
FISH
OCTOPUS
SALT
SHARK
STORM
TURTLE

74 - Agronomía

```
X Z G V E G E T A B L E S W H
N R Y R Z S U A W R H J I A I
G E G N O I T C U D O R P T S
T U O H M W O R G A N I C E Y
Y F L Y D U T S V E N J Z R S
X S O C P Z U H P E O W F O T
P W C A G R I C U L T U R E E
B L E I S E E D S D Z U B S M
P A A D E D I S E A S E S L S
D R N N O N O I T U L L O P N
R U R R T I C R Y E N E R G Y
P R Z T C S H E E R O S I O N
F E R T I L I Z E R I B J T O
S U S T A I N A B L E E P S B
E N V I R O N M E N T Z P Z G
```

AGRICULTURE	FERTILIZER
WATER	ENVIRONMENT
SCIENCE	ORGANIC
POLLUTION	PLANTS
GROWTH	PRODUCTION
ECOLOGY	RURAL
ENERGY	SEEDS
DISEASES	SYSTEMS
EROSION	SUSTAINABLE
STUDY	VEGETABLES

75 - Deporte

```
H  Z  K  U  H  Y  N  A  M  C  X  M  F  K  O
E  F  C  W  N  C  T  U  T  E  I  D  U  P  I
A  L  U  V  S  P  O  I  T  H  V  J  Z  D  W
L  G  B  O  D  Y  S  D  L  R  L  D  I  W  O
T  C  F  T  Y  V  W  N  T  I  I  E  Z  K  Z
H  Q  Q  H  F  N  I  Y  X  V  B  T  T  U  O
S  E  L  C  S  U  M  R  C  R  B  A  I  E  E
M  E  T  A  B  O  L  I  C  R  M  T  Q  O  C
F  I  V  O  N  G  L  F  C  N  N  B  S  D  N
B  G  Q  C  P  R  O  G  R  A  M  O  P  A  A
S  T  R  E  N  G  T  H  G  H  W  N  O  N  R
S  T  R  E  T  C  H  I  N  G  D  E  R  C  U
T  O  B  R  E  A  T  H  E  H  R  S  T  I  D
C  Y  C  L  I  N  G  I  I  K  J  J  S  N  N
M  A  X  I  M  I  Z  E  U  R  H  Q  O  G  E
```

ATHLETE	BONES
DANCING	MAXIMIZE
ABILITY	METABOLIC
CYCLING	MUSCLES
BODY	TO SWIM
SPORTS	NUTRITION
DIET	PROGRAM
COACH	ENDURANCE
STRETCHING	TO BREATHE
STRENGTH	HEALTH

76 - Actividades y Ocio

```
R E C C O S D P V S G G F T T
W E T S F O H N A Q N O S E R
Z Z L E H B G P A I I L U N A
Y V Z A O O B I T W N F H N V
R D I E X Z P V P F E T O I E
A B M X X I N P K L D R I S L
C B U S X V N G I K R A E N O
I H I K I N G G B N A S X Z G
N G H O X D A N A W G T O C N
G N I F R U S I S W L C S S I
F I S H I N G M E A L E Y C V
Z P S X J L Q M B H B S C B I
Q M P O V J J I A M Z X V B D
S A R T Y E S W L B O X I N G
Y C N A A D A S L P P I B B F
```

ART   GARDENING
BASEBALL   SWIMMING
BOXING   FISHING
DIVING   PAINTING
CAMPING   RELAXING
RACING   HIKING
SHOPPING   SURFING
SOCCER   TENNIS
GOLF   TRAVEL

77 - Ingeniería

```
O D F B Y S I X A S O Z Y S P
M Q I F P R T I U E V Q S T F
M W H A O E T A B X R U D R M
N T S F M V Z E B X K B E E E
O Y Q X Z E A N F I L X P N A
I S P M W L T L Q I L V T G S
T Z S J A R O E M W M I H T U
U D I A G R A M R T S N T H R
B I C A L C U L A T I O N Y E
I U E N I H C A M M B I H M M
R Q L N P K Q C A O V T U M E
T I G L E E H H W T Q C N J N
S L N Z K R X I R O S I Y O T
I L A F J R G K B R Y R I F V
D I E S E L A Y I J O F Q N Q
```

ANGLE
CALCULATION
DIAGRAM
DIAMETER
DIESEL
DISTRIBUTION
AXIS
ENERGY
STABILITY

FRICTION
STRENGTH
LIQUID
MACHINE
MEASUREMENT
MOTOR
LEVERS
DEPTH

78 - Comida #1

```
S  P  E  A  R  B  W  V  X  J  M  C  M  V  E
A  I  T  N  O  M  A  N  N  I  C  T  U  J  D
L  N  M  O  N  R  Y  R  A  G  U  S  G  J  Q
T  R  B  I  S  B  L  K  L  I  M  D  B  G  J
A  U  A  N  L  P  Q  O  F  E  C  I  U  J  R
E  T  S  O  W  Y  I  Z  Q  O  Y  D  W  F  B
M  Q  I  T  H  L  A  N  K  L  E  B  W  V  D
J  U  L  D  T  Q  U  E  A  C  I  H  Z  X  C
J  X  V  V  L  Y  X  F  H  C  I  L  R  A  G
S  T  R  A  W  B  E  R  R  Y  H  M  I  N  T
T  S  J  W  S  O  U  P  X  T  B  R  M  T  O
U  F  A  C  E  Y  W  M  C  M  C  W  H  G  R
N  J  O  L  L  C  R  A  W  P  T  U  Y  O  R
A  Z  I  U  A  U  F  X  P  J  P  Q  A  V  A
G  U  O  Z  N  D  L  E  M  O  N  O  O  X  C
```

GARLIC	STRAWBERRY
BASIL	JUICE
TUNA	MILK
SUGAR	LEMON
CINNAMON	MINT
MEAT	TURNIP
BARLEY	PEAR
ONION	SALT
SALAD	SOUP
SPINACH	CARROT

79 - Antigüedades

```
A  A  D  G  K  H  Z  G  G  J  T  S  J  R  S
S  U  A  I  S  E  D  A  C  E  D  Q  T  Z  Z
C  Z  T  S  V  U  H  L  U  S  Q  A  K  E  Q
U  G  N  H  Y  J  E  L  F  W  C  Q  C  N  E
L  C  E  S  E  G  V  E  U  N  U  S  U  A  L
P  E  M  T  R  N  I  R  Q  U  F  F  F  P  S
T  N  T  Y  U  L  T  Y  V  U  Z  M  G  R  X
U  T  S  L  T  R  A  I  W  A  A  U  C  I  S
R  U  E  E  I  U  R  F  C  X  L  L  G  C  A
E  R  V  N  N  M  O  S  K  Y  P  U  I  E  S
C  Y  N  T  R  D  C  Y  V  N  W  H  E  T  Q
R  E  I  E  U  A  E  L  E  G  A  N  T  X  Y
O  L  D  R  F  H  D  J  E  W  E  L  R  Y  G
C  O  I  N  S  A  U  C  T  I  O  N  T  D  P
R  E  S  T  O  R  A  T  I  O  N  F  Y  A  G
```

ART	INVESTMENT
AUTHENTIC	JEWELRY
QUALITY	COINS
DECORATIVE	FURNITURE
DECADES	PRICE
ELEGANT	RESTORATION
SCULPTURE	CENTURY
STYLE	AUCTION
GALLERY	VALUE
UNUSUAL	OLD

80 - Literatura

```
K B B Y G O L A N A W V H Z N
J I I D A P D Q N L J M D Z D
P O Q I P M M T T E M E H T B
N G S A U N C Q Y J C S Q Z K
O R A L S O Y K T S N D R X S
V A N O S I R A P M O C O Z Y
E P W G A S O Y B E I I H T D
L H S U U T D S O T T P H E E
R Y I E T L A S B P C E A D G
F H S M H C R C L N I O T H A
I B Y J O N R R I D F P E P R
Y E L T R O A S T Y L E M B T
P D A C H C N I M T E T K Y F
R O N J O M R H Y M E O U P O
L O A D E S C R I P T I O N P
```

ANALOGY   FICTION
ANALYSIS   METAPHOR
ANECDOTE   NARRATOR
AUTHOR   NOVEL
BIOGRAPHY   POEM
COMPARISON   POETIC
CONCLUSION   RHYME
DESCRIPTION   RHYTHM
DIALOGUE   THEME
STYLE   TRAGEDY

81 - Química

```
C C G P A E M G E O Z W N S T
C H S U H V E Y N X N O U B A
A K L H L L A O Z Y T G C Y V
T A A O S A L T Y G A A L Y E
A I T O R U T B M E S S E R A
L W E A L I U Y E N R I A H L
Y L M N R D N A S O D H R R K
S N W R Y N O E C I S Y J E A
T C A R B O N Z O I U D Z A L
U W S P D R W F S B D R A C I
S J A J Q T H G I E W O S T N
U F Z M T C F F X L A G L I E
B Q T B V E I Y J M H E M O V
D I U Q I L M L K R D N B N W
E N I A B E L U C E L O M B B
```

ALKALINE   ION
ACID   LIQUID
HEAT   METALS
CARBON   MOLECULE
CATALYST   NUCLEAR
CHLORINE   OXYGEN
ELECTRON   WEIGHT
ENZYME   REACTION
GAS   SALT
HYDROGEN

82 - Gobierno

```
C  I  T  I  Z  E  N  S  H  I  P  S  D  L  L
I  N  D  E  P  E  N  D  E  N  C  E  I  A  I
M  X  V  L  A  N  O  I  T  A  N  M  S  I  B
N  O  I  T  U  T  I  T  S  N  O  C  C  A  E
J  S  N  F  U  S  T  U  C  L  X  D  U  E  R
U  U  P  U  U  W  A  L  I  R  U  J  S  Z  T
L  F  D  E  M  Q  N  Y  T  A  J  D  S  N  Y
L  D  F  I  E  E  U  C  I  Q  U  I  I  S  A
I  A  A  F  C  C  N  A  L  R  S  S  O  O  L
I  E  O  U  I  I  H  T  O  T  T  T  N  X  S
P  L  C  M  L  A  A  S  P  C  I  R  D  C  T
X  V  R  E  D  A  E  L  P  I  C  I  R  R  A
D  E  M  O  C  R  A  C  Y  V  E  C  Y  M  T
E  Q  U  A  L  I  T  Y  Y  I  S  T  P  W  E
U  U  L  H  W  U  A  G  U  L  O  B  M  Y  S
```

CITIZENSHIP   JUDICIAL
CIVIL   JUSTICE
CONSTITUTION   LAW
DEMOCRACY   LIBERTY
SPEECH   LEADER
DISCUSSION   MONUMENT
DISTRICT   NATIONAL
STATE   NATION
EQUALITY   POLITICS
INDEPENDENCE   SYMBOL

83 - Creatividad

```
V Z Y T I S N E T N I W L F D
I M T W F M E G A M I Y A L R
S Q I V Y R P N M J C U S U A
I N R F S H U R S T E T K I M
O F A R N N R P E A U G I D A
N V L A O Y K D H S T F L I T
S P C T I S X X V W S I L T I
S P O N T A N E O U S I O Y C
S X B L O E T G L H L V O N U
A Q G M M N N O I T I U T N I
E X P R E S S I O N L P U I K
D I M A G I N A T I O N A Y D
I I N S P I R A T I O N B S Y
A U T H E N T I C I T Y E W Y
I N V E N T I V E G C H T Y B
```

AUTHENTICITY
CLARITY
DRAMATIC
EMOTIONS
SPONTANEOUS
EXPRESSION
FLUIDITY
SKILL
IDEAS

IMAGE
IMAGINATION
IMPRESSION
INSPIRATION
INTENSITY
INTUITION
INVENTIVE
SENSATION
VISIONS

84 - Filantropía

```
Q S S W C S E H X X G K L O G
G R O U P S L A O G L N L Y E
N R A N M M K W C N B A G N N
J F I V L A T E O D E E N L E
Y Y R S P R H S N V C S E I R
B O C X E G U C T X N D T R O
U U U L Q O M H A U A N A Y S
X C S T W R A I C K N U N V I
C I F X H P N L T X I F O H T
G L O B A L I D S T F V D A Y
U B T O Q L T R H I S T O R Y
B U Y F F L Y E L P O E P C P
P P Z J L O Z N O I S S I M U
C O M M U N I T Y T I R A H C
H G F F N A L E W V B Y U G G
```

CHARITY
COMMUNITY
CONTACTS
DONATE
FINANCE
FUNDS
GENEROSITY
PEOPLE
GLOBAL
GROUPS

HISTORY
HONESTY
HUMANITY
YOUTH
GOALS
MISSION
NEED
CHILDREN
PROGRAMS
PUBLIC

85 - Comida #2

```
G  D  X  U  B  T  T  V  Z  H  R  A  D  Y  T
J  I  A  G  T  L  E  F  N  W  H  E  A  T  O
W  W  N  C  H  E  R  R  Y  S  C  G  E  N  M
S  I  A  G  W  E  K  O  H  C  I  T  R  A  A
B  K  N  W  E  L  P  P  A  C  L  C  B  L  T
E  Z  A  S  V  R  N  E  K  C  I  H  C  P  O
K  Q  B  U  O  C  O  U  F  I  Y  E  C  G  J
A  F  D  N  O  M  L  A  W  O  U  E  T  G  T
J  E  J  F  G  R  A  P  E  H  N  S  K  E  A
G  T  O  L  N  Y  M  V  O  S  A  E  E  L  R
E  C  I  O  C  H  O  C  O  L  A  T  E  J  S
Y  G  A  W  S  G  X  J  A  E  Z  A  R  Q  F
M  Y  G  E  C  I  R  V  I  M  N  M  F  J  P
C  Q  T  R  U  G  O  Y  Y  W  R  Y  C  R  F
R  C  E  L  E  R  Y  V  T  Y  O  G  J  L  R
```

ARTICHOKE	KIWI
ALMOND	APPLE
CELERY	BREAD
RICE	BANANA
EGGPLANT	CHICKEN
CHERRY	CHEESE
CHOCOLATE	TOMATO
SUNFLOWER	WHEAT
EGG	GRAPE
GINGER	YOGURT

86 - Arte

```
S C T S H S P S J Y M O O D P
U O P S O T Y E I R U A X G K
B M K G N T A M R M P G N E V
J P G N E M R M B S P Y R R C
E L L I S S T S J O O L H U O
C E E T T I R G O R L N E T M
T X E N O L O G Z B A S A P P
M F E I C A P R R Y N Z V L O
C R E A T E E R U G I F I U S
I N S P I R E D L Z G W S C I
M L W B O R C H M W I B U S T
A P B P U U C X V Q R G A K I
R W Y B T S Z F D C O G L L O
E D Y Z A P O E T R Y Z V D N
C E X P R E S S I O N J Z H T
```

CERAMIC
COMPLEX
COMPOSITION
CREATE
SCULPTURE
EXPRESSION
FIGURE
HONEST
MOOD
INSPIRED

ORIGINAL
PERSONAL
PAINTINGS
POETRY
PORTRAY
SIMPLE
SYMBOL
SURREALISM
SUBJECT
VISUAL

87 - Diplomacia

```
R  Y  U  D  M  Z  J  K  K  Y  Q  E  G  B  R
P  W  X  G  M  J  U  V  B  P  J  C  S  V  E
A  O  Q  J  T  W  S  E  T  H  I  C  S  Q  S
C  D  L  X  C  I  T  A  M  O  L  P  I  D  O
C  O  V  I  N  O  I  S  S  U  C  S  I  D  L
O  F  M  I  T  D  C  F  E  I  D  G  D  I  U
O  O  F  M  S  I  E  E  M  B  A  S  S  Y  T
P  R  V  O  U  E  C  F  P  D  Q  C  S  T  I
E  E  A  E  V  N  R  S  I  R  H  O  O  I  O
R  I  E  E  L  O  I  I  X  Z  D  N  L  R  N
A  G  J  E  G  G  L  T  L  H  O  F  U  U  D
T  N  Q  J  Z  H  Z  Y  Y  G  I  L  T  C  M
I  G  O  V  E  R  N  M  E  N  T  I  I  E  M
O  I  N  T  E  G  R  I  T  Y  H  C  O  S  Q
N  L  A  N  G  U  A  G  E  S  Q  T  N  P  P
```

ADVISER	GOVERNMENT
COMMUNITY	LANGUAGES
CONFLICT	INTEGRITY
COOPERATION	JUSTICE
DIPLOMATIC	POLITICS
DISCUSSION	RESOLUTION
EMBASSY	SECURITY
FOREIGN	SOLUTION
ETHICS	

88 - Herboristería

```
L A V E N D E R A P P R J B T
C N V X P S I X R A G L U L Q
D U G N T U Z F O R R I A E H
C I L R A G B L M S E S D N T
K I L I E P X O A L E A W N T
E S B L N P E W T E N B S E W
P S U N Q A H E I Y F Z N F N
F L A V O R R R C X A V G J O
F H Y Q Q L H Y R A M E S O R
M Z C Q U A L I T Y W O V X F
M A R J O R A M N E D R A G F
A E Q F P P U A I J N Q K Q A
L Q D E Z A W S M N V F B Q S
I N G R E D I E N T R E T X P
F E I T A R R A G O N Q Y P C
```

GARLIC	INGREDIENT
BASIL	GARDEN
AROMATIC	LAVENDER
SAFFRON	MARJORAM
QUALITY	MINT
CULINARY	PARSLEY
DILL	PLANT
TARRAGON	ROSEMARY
FLOWER	FLAVOR
FENNEL	GREEN

89 - Energía

```
I  G  E  T  G  A  S  O  L  I  N  E  T  S  U
N  D  L  E  U  F  S  T  E  A  M  H  H  U  W
D  N  E  G  O  R  D  Y  H  K  P  G  E  N  K
U  I  C  W  B  A  B  W  H  L  D  X  F  A  F
S  W  T  G  I  F  L  I  H  L  F  G  E  D  T
T  G  R  S  Y  U  E  V  N  O  T  O  H  P  B
R  Q  O  E  U  S  V  H  E  P  N  Y  E  M
Y  N  N  U  L  N  E  L  B  A  W  E  N  E  R
P  O  L  L  U  T  I  O  N  C  H  N  U  A  D
F  X  Y  E  L  L  D  E  L  E  C  T  R  I  C
M  J  B  A  T  T  E  R  Y  J  O  Y  L  S  D
N  O  B  R  A  C  W  S  U  V  A  J  Q  F  T
F  F  T  S  D  D  I  S  G  Z  A  V  N  O  G
L  Y  P  O  R  T  N  E  H  L  Y  P  N  T  P
C  I  B  G  R  A  E  L  C  U  N  B  K  E  Y
```

BATTERY	GASOLINE
HEAT	HYDROGEN
CARBON	INDUSTRY
FUEL	MOTOR
POLLUTION	NUCLEAR
DIESEL	RENEWABLE
ELECTRON	SUN
ELECTRIC	TURBINE
ENTROPY	STEAM
PHOTON	WIND

90 - Insectos

```
B U T T E R F L Y C K V Q W G
D R G Z Z V G I Z W I B H A S
T E N R O H T A S S T C C S G
N C S N A E L F T Z E D A P V
A W D N C S Y N S C R M O D G
O T E U L V S J U G M A R I A
J H I P D D N H C W I N K H P
Z W P F R C J T O W T T C P J
L A R V A C C O L P E I O A Y
N E V D T A Z M A B P S C C B
Y L F N O G A R D Q E E B M G
F T D V A A B O Y I P E R M N
M P F E R E Z W B K Y V T E G
V N Z T P O T I U Q S O M L G
M Y E S R A H X G C U Z E E E
```

BEE
WASP
HORNET
APHID
CICADA
COCKROACH
BEETLE
WORM
ANT
LOCUST

LARVA
DRAGONFLY
MANTIS
BUTTERFLY
LADYBUG
MOSQUITO
MOTH
FLEA
GRASSHOPPER
TERMITE

91 - Especias

```
W W P Q B R O N V A N I L L A
F L E C I R O C I L G A R Q D
A E K E T H M U E M X B W U N
A N V U T J R F M K U X G K U
S V I L E N N E F Q Q C W T N
Z K A S R S Y V P A P R I K A
T G R K E O N O I Q I V J G U
S W E E T U Y L R Y Q L Y I N
S S P N G R S C I L R A G N U
A R P X A O I A N W Q O V G T
L W E L W V E J F S G N D E M
T C P L N A T H K F A U P R E
O N I O N L N A N Y R R U C G
W B Y Q Q F W S S Q M O S H N
W C I N N A M O N M Z K N R O
```

SOUR
GARLIC
BITTER
ANISE
SAFFRON
CINNAMON
ONION
CLOVE
CUMIN
CURRY

SWEET
FENNEL
GINGER
NUTMEG
PAPRIKA
PEPPER
LICORICE
FLAVOR
SALT
VANILLA

92 - Emociones

```
C L Q F E A W B F Q R G Z G K
G O O Q Y N Z J E Q E R G V X
R A N V Y G A C I C L A L L D
T U P T E E T P L M A T E W S
M I S N E R S F E L X E U Y P
Z Z U G K N P S R A E F P T S
P Z U B O W T N V C D U G I G
S U R P R I S E X O W L E L W
J O Y B L I S S E N D N I K
W M S A T I S F I E D P K U D
C I C T S Y M P A T H Y I Q H
R S G U C B O R E D O M V N G
T E N D E R N E S S T V D A I
D E M B A R R A S S E D B R V
S A D N E S S F M Z F I V T F
```

BOREDOM	ANGER
GRATEFUL	FEAR
JOY	PEACE
RELIEF	RELAXED
LOVE	SATISFIED
EMBARRASSED	SYMPATHY
BLISS	SURPRISE
KINDNESS	TENDERNESS
CALM	TRANQUILITY
CONTENT	SADNESS

93 - Jazz

```
I  V  T  L  A  T  A  U  T  R  I  C  F  L  O
F  E  R  A  D  P  M  B  M  H  M  O  A  F  L
Z  C  E  U  L  A  W  J  Q  Y  P  M  V  E  G
P  A  C  O  O  E  L  S  K  T  R  P  O  E  D
E  R  N  E  G  L  N  B  W  H  O  O  R  H  A
U  T  O  L  B  Y  C  T  U  M  V  S  I  R  W
Q  S  C  U  F  T  P  M  R  M  I  E  T  D  Z
I  E  R  U  C  S  S  Z  J  N  S  R  E  V  A
N  H  T  N  F  U  N  Z  U  L  A  D  S  A  R
H  C  J  E  R  O  R  I  W  C  T  X  H  Y  T
C  R  N  W  S  M  R  Y  R  I  I  L  H  D  I
E  O  K  X  G  A  T  E  G  N  O  S  R  R  S
T  O  D  K  E  F  D  P  D  S  N  C  U  U  T
E  M  P  H  A  S  I  S  G  B  V  D  N  M  J
C  O  M  P  O  S  I  T  I  O  N  N  R  S  X
```

ARTIST	GENRE
ALBUM	IMPROVISATION
SONG	MUSIC
COMPOSITION	NEW
COMPOSER	ORCHESTRA
CONCERT	RHYTHM
STYLE	TALENT
EMPHASIS	DRUMS
FAMOUS	TECHNIQUE
FAVORITES	OLD

94 - Mediciones

```
B M A R G O Z B N Z L T K H L
Y Q E T D E J J O S H W B R E
T I Q T K D E P T H C N I E N
E Z D T E E C R H E I G H T G
T C E Q Y R N R G W E M T E T
R P T B J V U A I E A Y D M H
K M H F C I O X E E D X I I F
E K G N M O P R W C N M W T L
L H L N P L W D Y D I A N N I
Q K M A R G O L I K N S S E T
K I L O M E T E R V C S M C E
A W L L X I M I N U T E R J R
V O L U M E C I X B V E L M F
G R M O B L L E G R L L C B A
E B W Q A E L O D J I L P O S
```

HEIGHT   LENGTH
WIDTH   MASS
BYTE   METER
CENTIMETER   MINUTE
DECIMAL   OUNCE
DEGREE   WEIGHT
GRAM   DEPTH
KILOGRAM   INCH
KILOMETER   TON
LITER   VOLUME

95 - Barcos

```
N Y S S G P A E M I T I R A M
A A Z E R Y Y O U B S I N C E
U C O A D O A N J M A L D R I
T H U I U J H A R Q M R E E P
I T J S U R N C F M B U F V M
C Y C I Z C C U N E Z V K I R
A U D G H N P A K A K X L R Z
L B P B X K R W E N G I N E B
U F H M A W F W P E E O Z M B
J K J K J R X H O L B W W C R
H M E C A D U W R L A K E I A
C R W Q H Y R R E F M W B L F
L Y K L J T A O B L I A S D T
O C E A N F M K S A I L O R Y
J T C R E W L N M Q V F R O H
```

ANCHOR
RAFT
BUOY
CANOE
ROPE
FERRY
KAYAK
LAKE
SEA
TIDE

SAILOR
MARITIME
MAST
ENGINE
NAUTICAL
OCEAN
RIVER
CREW
SAILBOAT
YACHT

96 - Antártida

```
P R E T A W A L P T G T N F S
E X E D G C I F I T N E I C S
N B X S Y T O W B N I M T M L
G U Y U E W N Z I Z S P I I A
U C K O V A T R J S L E P G R
I U O M E E R C E X A R E R E
N M P N H C S C T O N A N A N
S K R R T I L L H V D T I T I
W U X X F I W O M E S U N I M
C H R B X U N U U Y R R S O Y
Y H P A R G O E G D A E U N S
B A Y S R C S C N U S B L R B
G L A C I E R S M T E X A R T
C O N S E R V A T I O N F J N
C K F R R O C K Y B I R D S F
```

WATER	ISLANDS
BAY	MIGRATION
SCIENTIFIC	MINERALS
CONSERVATION	CLOUDS
CONTINENT	BIRDS
GEOGRAPHY	PENINSULA
GLACIERS	PENGUINS
ICE	ROCKY
RESEARCHER	TEMPERATURE

97 - Mamíferos

```
P  L  W  C  A  T  E  S  D  S  D  B  X  Y  V
K  U  M  X  S  I  K  H  B  D  O  G  E  N  J
C  A  O  M  O  B  S  E  T  O  Y  O  C  A  X
B  K  N  J  Q  B  Z  E  B  R  E  T  X  V  R
R  M  T  G  V  A  P  Y  E  K  N  O  M  E  E
P  K  U  Q  A  R  H  U  I  G  N  A  F  D  N
N  W  J  W  W  R  A  U  U  I  O  H  X  N  R
G  T  W  O  C  S  O  H  P  R  D  P  S  P  R
D  O  N  L  Z  J  D  O  B  A  K  E  L  U  T
O  V  R  F  H  O  R  S  E  F  T  L  Y  T  G
L  Z  N  I  A  Z  S  E  Q  F  S  E  E  W  P
P  D  I  E  L  A  H  W  L  E  R  A  C  G  I
H  O  B  G  N  L  Z  E  B  R  A  I  U  Y  D
I  J  G  W  O  P  A  A  L  S  H  F  D  J  X
N  I  I  B  U  L  L  E  M  A  C  Q  O  E  N
```

WHALE	CAT
DONKEY	GORILLA
HORSE	GIRAFFE
CAMEL	WOLF
KANGAROO	MONKEY
ZEBRA	BEAR
RABBIT	SHEEP
COYOTE	DOG
DOLPHIN	BULL
ELEPHANT	FOX

98 - Boxeo

```
R  I  G  S  U  C  F  I  H  P  X  O  N  E  Y
E  O  F  G  T  O  O  P  H  L  C  E  H  R  C
T  J  P  N  U  R  C  G  L  O  V  E  S  D  R
H  X  I  E  W  N  U  I  R  Q  Y  T  F  X  W
G  J  B  G  S  E  S  N  E  W  Z  U  D  G  K
I  M  Z  D  I  R  F  J  C  A  A  H  Q  T  R
F  C  T  T  L  R  G  U  O  A  C  H  I  N  E
R  E  F  E  R  E  E  R  V  Q  P  T  B  E  X
A  K  K  P  H  F  H  I  E  U  B  G  V  N  H
I  U  C  I  O  M  Y  E  R  R  C  N  F  O  A
B  E  L  L  C  I  K  S  Y  T  N  E  W  P  U
S  K  I  L  L  K  N  W  D  Y  P  R  T  P  S
Q  U  I  C  K  G  P  T  H  Y  T  T  Z  O  T
Z  F  I  S  T  E  L  L  S  B  B  S  Q  Y  E
B  O  D  Y  Z  U  E  L  B  O  W  S  X  E  D
```

REFEREE	GLOVES
CHIN	SKILL
BELL	INJURIES
FOCUS	FIGHTER
ELBOW	OPPONENT
ROPES	KICK
BODY	POINTS
CORNER	FIST
EXHAUSTED	QUICK
STRENGTH	RECOVERY

99 - Abejas

```
B V X C Z C H J S F U K X Q I
B Y N B H W I P J L R O X O Q
V S U N Z Q V L B O C G P V O
F O O D Y U E A L W C S O W F
N I T D P E I N O E J X L K L
T C I P Q E W T S R F R L E B
X I U I N N E S S S B O E C E
G A R D E N S Y O L C T N O N
S V F W A X F M M O S A O S E
I N S E C T D R O Q S N D Y F
A Z R C H R X A O K F I X S I
Y T L D J X I W E U E L U T C
W I N G S M A S W Y T L N E I
D I V E R S I T Y E N O H M A
C Y O I D T L C U H Y P J K L
```

WINGS	FRUIT
BENEFICIAL	SMOKE
WAX	INSECT
HIVE	GARDEN
FOOD	HONEY
DIVERSITY	PLANTS
ECOSYSTEM	POLLEN
SWARM	POLLINATOR
BLOSSOM	QUEEN
FLOWERS	SUN

100 - Psicología

```
P E R C E P T I O N B U S U A
T H O U G H T S X W C F E N V
D T N E M S S E S S A U N C D
N N C H I L D H O O D G S O H
S U O I C S N O C B U S A N T
U Y T I L A N O S R E P T S B
G X Z O H F X W O Y V L I C E
F T N E M T N I O P P A O I H
Y P C D E G O O I A E C N O A
T B A A R M U L C R O I E U V
I D E A S E Q A Q E U N J S I
L S T F Y A A J N H Q I U F O
A S N O I T O M E T S L K S R
E P R O B L E M S O Y C O G R
R C O G N I T I O N Y Y H N N
```

APPOINTMENT   CHILDHOOD
CLINICAL   THOUGHTS
COGNITION   PERCEPTION
BEHAVIOR   PERSONALITY
CONFLICT   PROBLEM
EGO   REALITY
EMOTIONS   SENSATION
ASSESSMENT   SUBCONSCIOUS
IDEAS   DREAMS
UNCONSCIOUS   THERAPY

1 - Arqueología

2 - Granja #2

3 - Mueble

4 - Aviones

5 - Tipos de Cabello

6 - Ética

7 - Ciencia Ficción

8 - Granja #1

9 - Camping

10 - Fruta

11 - Geología

12 - Álgebra

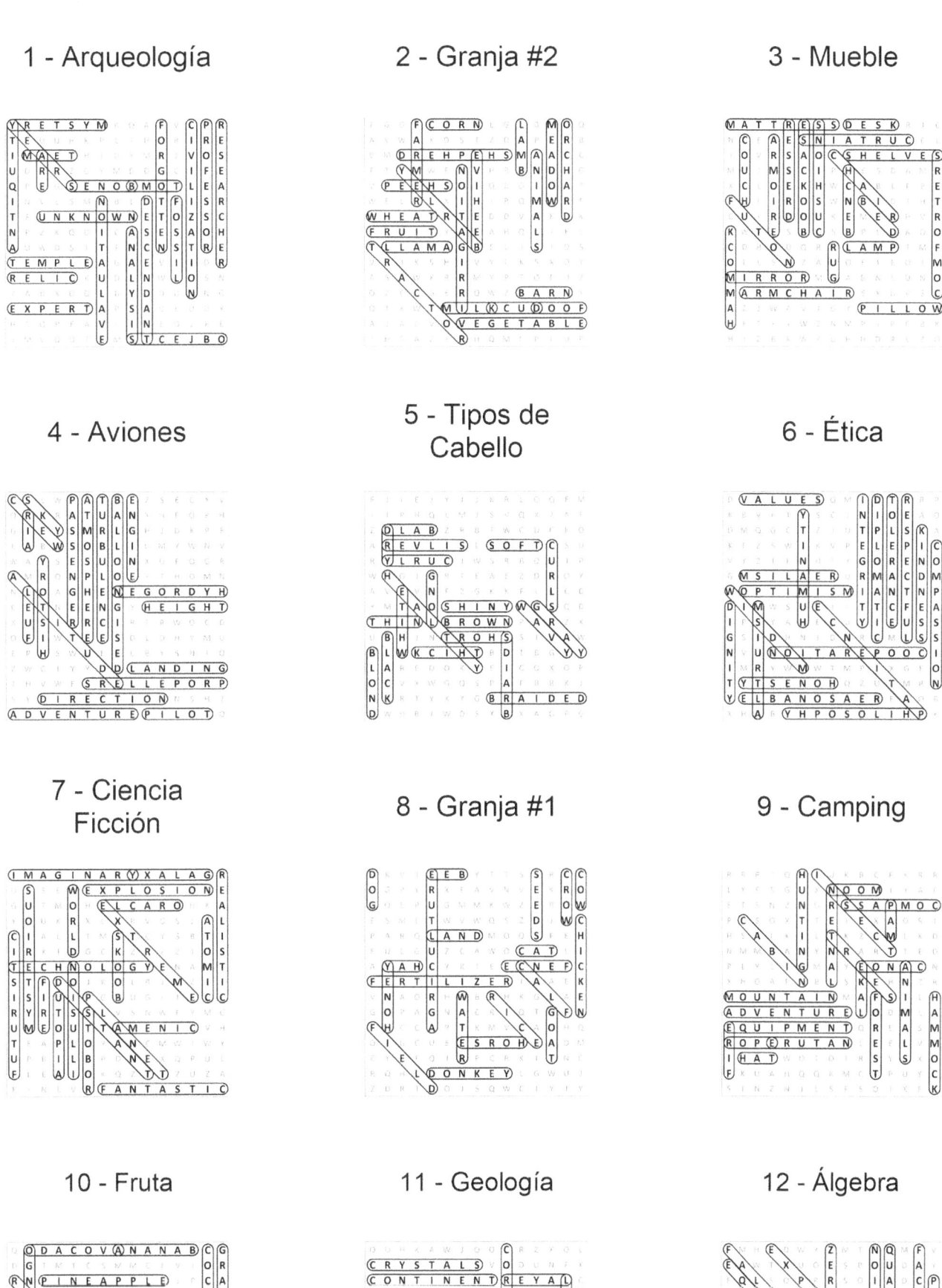

13 - Plantas

14 - Suministros de Arte

15 - Negocio

16 - Jardín

17 - Países #2

18 - Números

19 - Física

20 - Belleza

21 - Países #1

22 - Mitología

23 - Ecología

24 - Casa

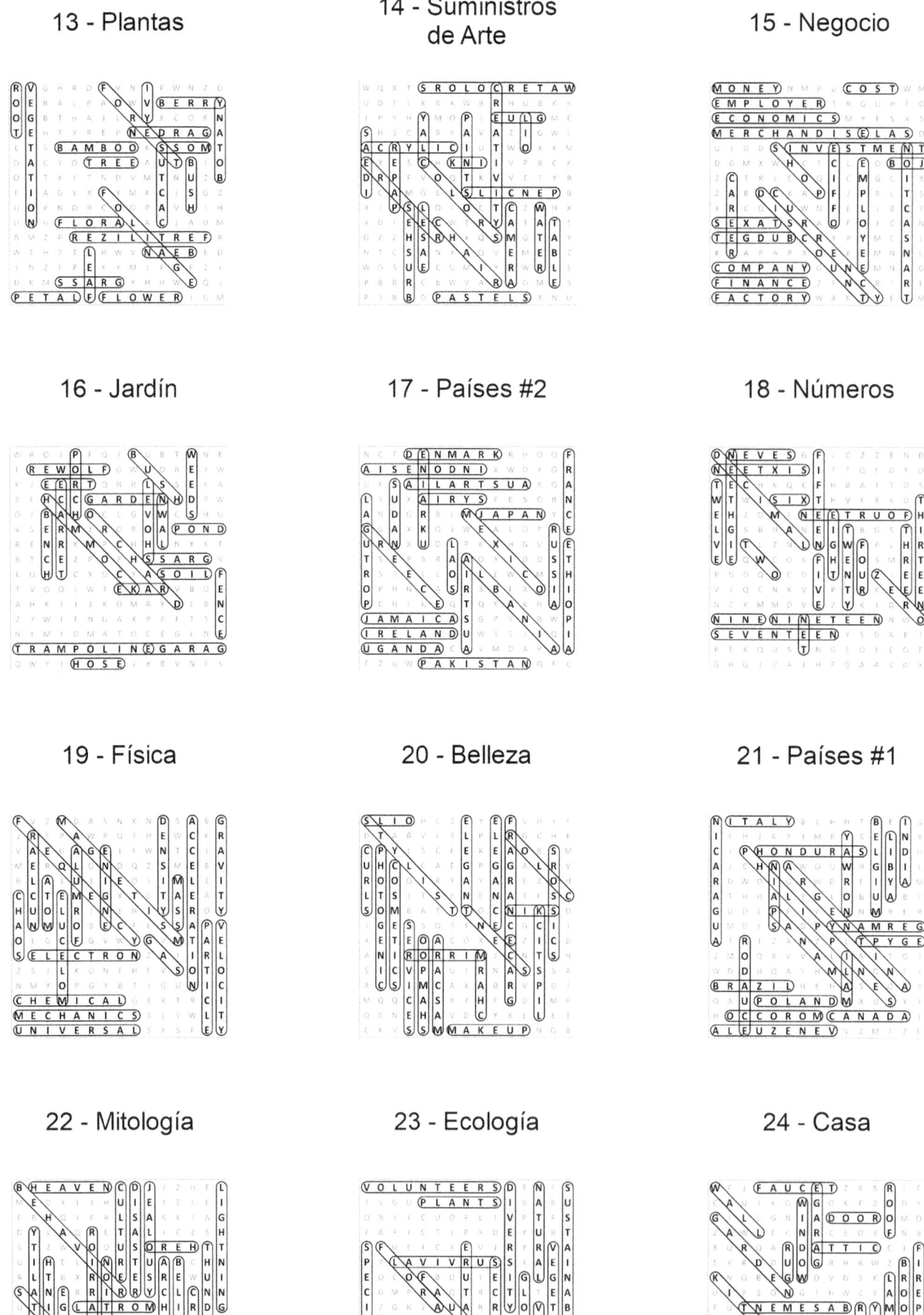

25 - Salud y Bienestar #2

HEALTHY · WEIGHT · DESSERTS · INFECTION · VITAMINS · HOSPITAL · RECOVERY · GREEN · HYGIENE · MASSAGE · ANATOMY · NUTRITION · DISEASE

26 - Selva Tropical

RESTORATION · JUNGLE · AMPHIBIAN · INDIGENOUS · PRESERVATION · BOTANICAL · BLOSSOM · CLOUDS · NATURE · MAMMALS · INSECTS

27 - Colores

WHITE · ORANGE · PURPLE · YELLOW · BLUE · BROWN · MAGENTA · RED · BLACK · BEIGE · SEPIA · VIOLET · CRIMSON · PINK · FUCHSIA

28 - Adjetivos #1

AROMATIC · INTERESTING · NATURAL · VALUABLE · HONEST · HUGE · TIRED · HEAVY · MODERN · CURIOUS · PERFECT · YOUNG

29 - Familia

GRANDSON · NEPHEW · NIECE · MOTHER · BROTHER · MATERNAL · DAUGHTER · CHILDREN · COUSIN · CHILD

30 - Disciplinas Científicas

ASTRONOMY · COMMUNICATION · ARCHAEOLOGY · CHEMISTRY · GEOLOGY · SOCIOLOGY · PHYSIOLOGY · BOTANY

31 - Cocina

OVEN · NAPKIN · FOOD · TOAST · SPICES · KETTLE · REFRIGERATOR · CHOPSTICKS · KNIVES · FREEZER · BOWL · GRILL · SPOONS

32 - Moda

MODERN · LACE · PATTERN · BUTTON · EXPENSIVE · BRACELET · CLOTHING · ELEGANT · PRACTICAL · TEXTURE

33 - Electricidad

NETWORK · NEGATIVE · LASER · QUANTITY · EQUIPMENT · GENERATOR · BATTERY · BULB · WIRE · SOCKET · POSITIVE · ELECTRICIAN · TELEPHONE · LAMP

34 - Salud y Bienestar #1

SKIN · ACTIVE · HEIGHT · DOCTOR · RELAXATION · TREATMENT · MUSCLES · HABIT

35 - Adjetivos #2

PRODUCTIVE · FRESH · SALTY · NORMAL · RESPONSIBLE · DESCRIPTIVE · EDIBLE · PROUD · INTERESTING · FAMOUS · STRONG · ELEGANT · SPICY · TIRED

36 - Cuerpo Humano

TONGUE · BRAIN · FACE · EYES · NOSE · FINGER · SHOULDER · ANKLE · KNEE · SKIN · HEART · CHIN

37 - Calentamiento Gl

38 - Ciencia

39 - Restaurante #2

40 - Profesiones #1

41 - Geometría

42 - Baile

43 - Matemáticas

44 - Restaurante #1

45 - Profesiones #2

46 - Senderismo

47 - Naturaleza

48 - Conduciendo

49 - Ballet

50 - Fuerza y Gravedad

51 - Aventura

52 - Pájaros

53 - Geografía

54 - Música

55 - Enfermedad

56 - Actividades

57 - Instrumentos Musicales

58 - Formas

59 - Flores

60 - Astronomía

61 - Paisajes

62 - Días y Meses

63 - Biología

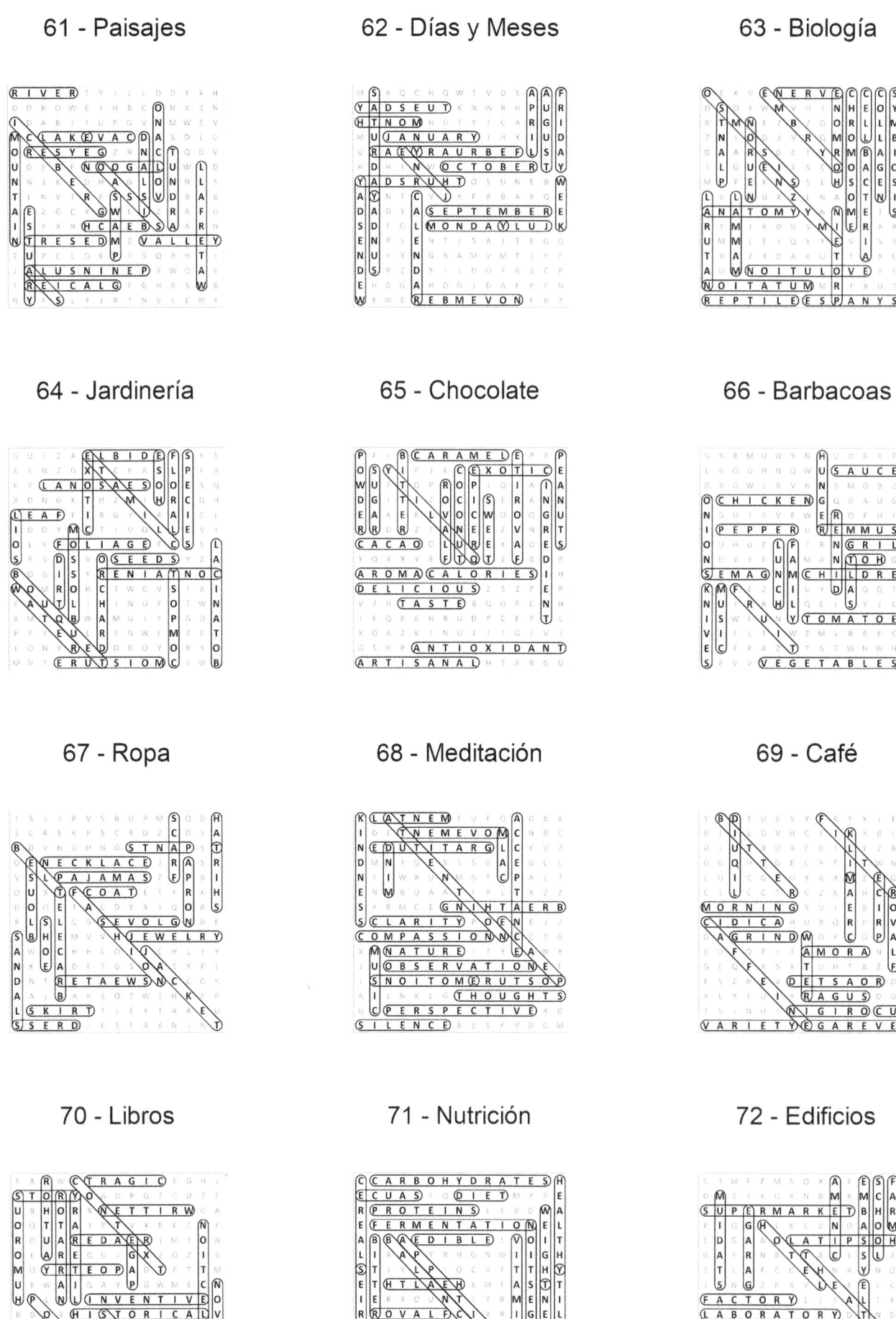

64 - Jardinería

65 - Chocolate

66 - Barbacoas

67 - Ropa

68 - Meditación

69 - Café

70 - Libros

71 - Nutrición

72 - Edificios

73 - Océano

74 - Agronomía

75 - Deporte

76 - Actividades y Ocio

77 - Ingeniería

78 - Comida #1

79 - Antigüedades

80 - Literatura

81 - Química

82 - Gobierno

83 - Creatividad

84 - Filantropía

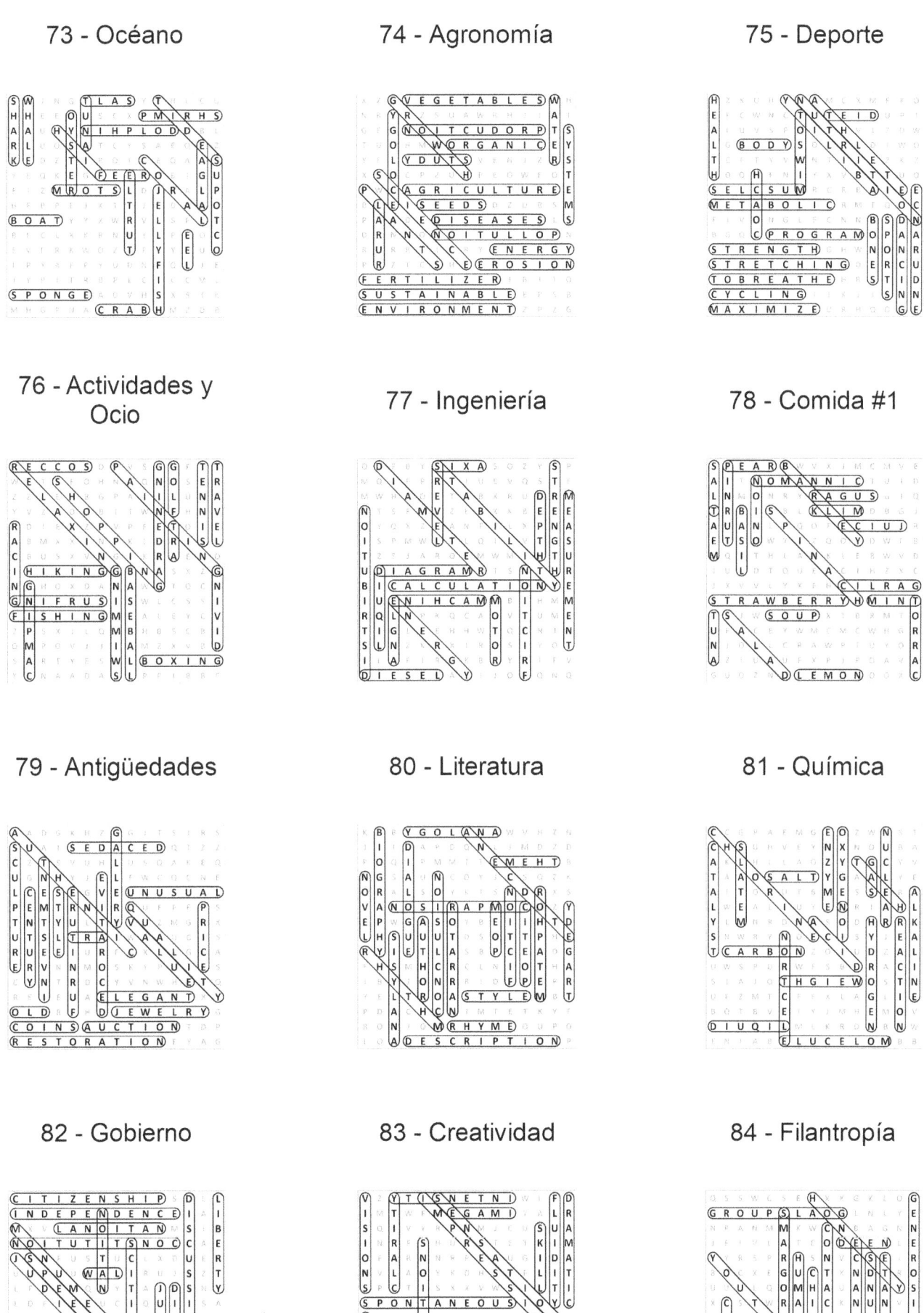

85 - Comida #2

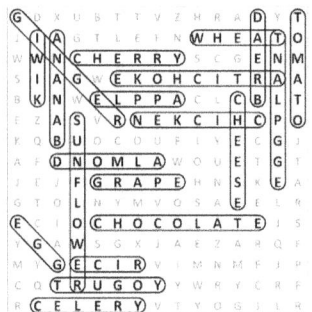

86 - Arte

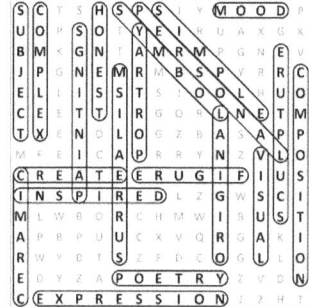

87 - Diplomacia

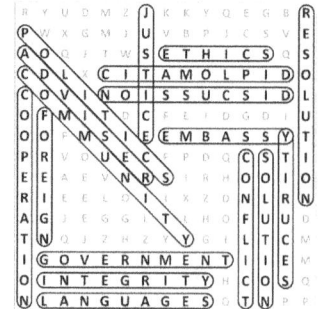

88 - Herboristería

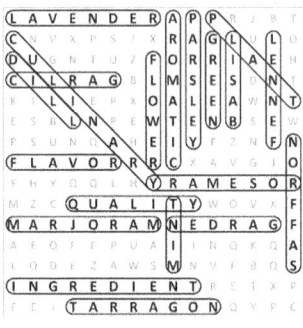

89 - Energía

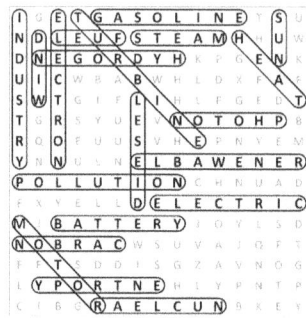

90 - Insectos

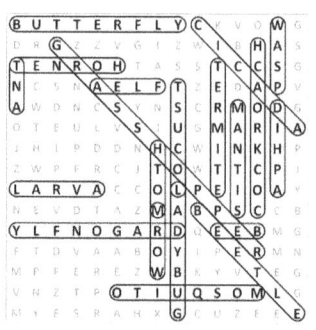

91 - Especias

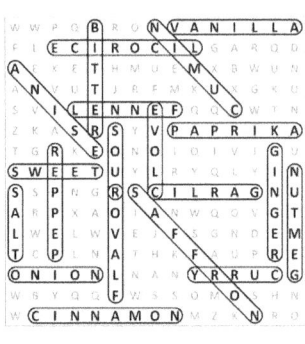

92 - Emociones

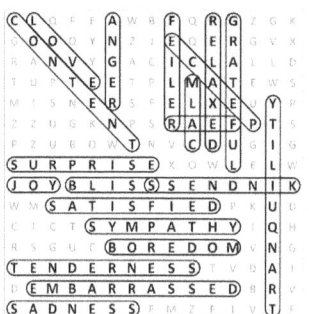

93 - Jazz

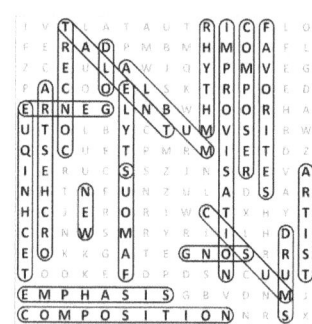

94 - Mediciones

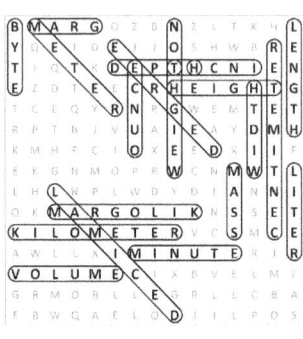

95 - Barcos

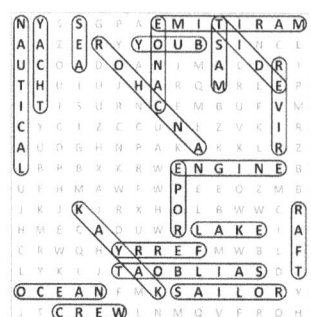

96 - Antártida

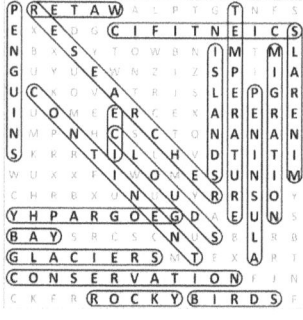

97 - Mamíferos

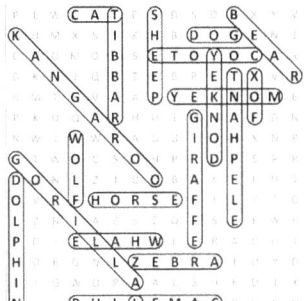

98 - Boxeo

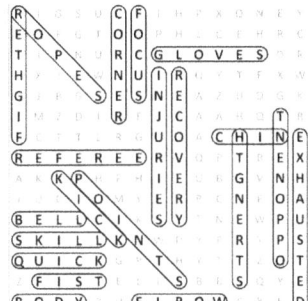

99 - Abejas

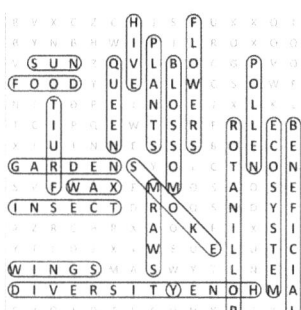

100 - Psicología

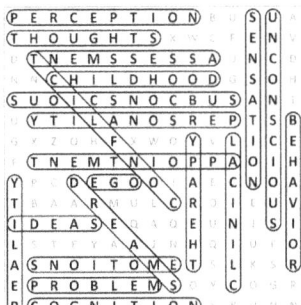

Diccionario

Abejas
Bees

Alas	Wings
Beneficioso	Beneficial
Cera	Wax
Colmena	Hive
Comida	Food
Diversidad	Diversity
Ecosistema	Ecosystem
Enjambre	Swarm
Flor	Blossom
Flores	Flowers
Fruta	Fruit
Humo	Smoke
Insecto	Insect
Jardín	Garden
Miel	Honey
Plantas	Plants
Polen	Pollen
Polinizador	Pollinator
Reina	Queen
Sol	Sun

Actividades
Activities

Actividad	Activity
Arte	Art
Artesanía	Crafts
Caza	Hunting
Cerámica	Ceramics
Costura	Sewing
Fotografía	Photography
Habilidad	Skill
Intereses	Interests
Jardinería	Gardening
Juegos	Games
Lectura	Reading
Magia	Magic
Ocio	Leisure
Pesca	Fishing
Pintura	Painting
Placer	Pleasure
Relajación	Relaxation
Rompecabezas	Puzzles
Senderismo	Hiking

Actividades y Ocio
Activities and Leisure

Arte	Art
Baloncesto	Basketball
Béisbol	Baseball
Boxeo	Boxing
Buceo	Diving
Camping	Camping
Carreras	Racing
Compras	Shopping
Fútbol	Soccer
Golf	Golf
Jardinería	Gardening
Natación	Swimming
Pesca	Fishing
Pintura	Painting
Relajante	Relaxing
Senderismo	Hiking
Surf	Surfing
Tenis	Tennis
Viaje	Travel
Voleibol	Volleyball

Adjetivos #1
Adjectives #1

Absoluto	Absolute
Activo	Active
Ambicioso	Ambitious
Aromático	Aromatic
Atractivo	Attractive
Brillante	Bright
Enorme	Huge
Generoso	Generous
Grande	Large
Honesto	Honest
Importante	Important
Inocente	Innocent
Joven	Young
Lento	Slow
Moderno	Modern
Oscuro	Dark
Perfecto	Perfect
Pesado	Heavy
Serio	Serious
Valioso	Valuable

Adjetivos #2
Adjectives #2

Cansado	Tired
Comestible	Edible
Creativo	Creative
Descriptivo	Descriptive
Dramático	Dramatic
Elegante	Elegant
Famoso	Famous
Fresco	Fresh
Fuerte	Strong
Interesante	Interesting
Natural	Natural
Normal	Normal
Nuevo	New
Orgulloso	Proud
Picante	Spicy
Productivo	Productive
Responsable	Responsible
Salado	Salty
Saludable	Healthy
Seco	Dry

Agronomía
Agronomy

Agricultura	Agriculture
Agua	Water
Ciencia	Science
Contaminación	Pollution
Crecimiento	Growth
Ecología	Ecology
Energía	Energy
Enfermedades	Diseases
Erosión	Erosion
Estudio	Study
Fertilizante	Fertilizer
Medio Ambiente	Environment
Orgánico	Organic
Plantas	Plants
Producción	Production
Rural	Rural
Semillas	Seeds
Sistemas	Systems
Sostenible	Sustainable
Verduras	Vegetables

Antártida
Antarctica

Agua	Water
Bahía	Bay
Científico	Scientific
Conservación	Conservation
Continente	Continent
Expedición	Expedition
Geografía	Geography
Glaciares	Glaciers
Hielo	Ice
Investigador	Researcher
Islas	Islands
Migración	Migration
Minerales	Minerals
Nubes	Clouds
Pájaros	Birds
Península	Peninsula
Pingüinos	Penguins
Rocoso	Rocky
Temperatura	Temperature
Topografía	Topography

Antigüedades
Antiques

Arte	Art
Auténtico	Authentic
Calidad	Quality
Decorativo	Decorative
Décadas	Decades
Elegante	Elegant
Escultura	Sculpture
Estilo	Style
Galería	Gallery
Inusual	Unusual
Inversión	Investment
Joyas	Jewelry
Monedas	Coins
Mueble	Furniture
Precio	Price
Restauración	Restoration
Siglo	Century
Subasta	Auction
Valor	Value
Viejo	Old

Arqueología
Archeology

Análisis	Analysis
Antigüedad	Antiquity
Años	Years
Civilización	Civilization
Descendiente	Descendant
Desconocido	Unknown
Equipo	Team
Era	Era
Evaluación	Evaluation
Experto	Expert
Fósil	Fossil
Huesos	Bones
Investigador	Researcher
Misterio	Mystery
Objetos	Objects
Olvidado	Forgotten
Profesor	Professor
Reliquia	Relic
Templo	Temple
Tumba	Tomb

Arte
Art

Cerámica	Ceramic
Complejo	Complex
Composición	Composition
Crear	Create
Escultura	Sculpture
Expresión	Expression
Figura	Figure
Honesto	Honest
Humor	Mood
Inspirado	Inspired
Original	Original
Personal	Personal
Pinturas	Paintings
Poesía	Poetry
Retratar	Portray
Sencillo	Simple
Símbolo	Symbol
Surrealismo	Surrealism
Tema	Subject
Visual	Visual

Astronomía
Astronomy

Asteroide	Asteroid
Astronauta	Astronaut
Astrónomo	Astronomer
Cielo	Sky
Cohete	Rocket
Constelación	Constellation
Cosmos	Cosmos
Eclipse	Eclipse
Equinoccio	Equinox
Galaxia	Galaxy
Luna	Moon
Meteoro	Meteor
Observatorio	Observatory
Planeta	Planet
Radiación	Radiation
Satélite	Satellite
Supernova	Supernova
Telescopio	Telescope
Tierra	Earth
Universo	Universe

Aventura
Adventure

Actividad	Activity
Alegría	Joy
Amigos	Friends
Belleza	Beauty
Destino	Destination
Dificultad	Difficulty
Entusiasmo	Enthusiasm
Excursión	Excursion
Inusual	Unusual
Itinerario	Itinerary
Naturaleza	Nature
Navegación	Navigation
Nuevo	New
Oportunidad	Chance
Peligroso	Dangerous
Preparación	Preparation
Seguridad	Safety
Sorprendente	Surprising
Valentía	Bravery
Viajes	Travels

Aviones
Airplanes

Aire	Air
Altitud	Altitude
Altura	Height
Aterrizaje	Landing
Atmósfera	Atmosphere
Aventura	Adventure
Cielo	Sky
Combustible	Fuel
Construcción	Construction
Dirección	Direction
Diseño	Design
Globo	Balloon
Hélices	Propellers
Hidrógeno	Hydrogen
Historia	History
Motor	Engine
Pasajero	Passenger
Piloto	Pilot
Tripulación	Crew
Turbulencia	Turbulence

Álgebra
Algebra

Cantidad	Quantity
Cero	Zero
Diagrama	Diagram
División	Division
Ecuación	Equation
Exponente	Exponent
Factor	Factor
Falso	False
Fórmula	Formula
Fracción	Fraction
Infinito	Infinite
Lineal	Linear
Matriz	Matrix
Número	Number
Paréntesis	Parenthesis
Problema	Problem
Resta	Subtraction
Simplificar	Simplify
Solución	Solution
Variable	Variable

Baile
Dance

Academia	Academy
Alegre	Joyful
Arte	Art
Clásico	Classical
Coreografía	Choreography
Cuerpo	Body
Cultura	Culture
Cultural	Cultural
Emoción	Emotion
Ensayo	Rehearsal
Expresivo	Expressive
Gracia	Grace
Movimiento	Movement
Música	Music
Postura	Posture
Ritmo	Rhythm
Saltar	Jump
Socio	Partner
Tradicional	Traditional
Visual	Visual

Ballet
Ballet

Aplauso	Applause
Artístico	Artistic
Audiencia	Audience
Bailarina	Ballerina
Bailarines	Dancers
Compositor	Composer
Coreografía	Choreography
Ensayo	Rehearsal
Estilo	Style
Expresivo	Expressive
Gesto	Gesture
Habilidad	Skill
Intensidad	Intensity
Lecciones	Lessons
Músculos	Muscles
Música	Music
Orquesta	Orchestra
Práctica	Practice
Ritmo	Rhythm
Técnica	Technique

Barbacoas
Barbecues

Almuerzo	Lunch
Caliente	Hot
Cebollas	Onions
Cena	Dinner
Cuchillos	Knives
Ensaladas	Salads
Familia	Family
Fruta	Fruit
Hambre	Hunger
Juegos	Games
Música	Music
Niños	Children
Parrilla	Grill
Pimienta	Pepper
Pollo	Chicken
Sal	Salt
Salsa	Sauce
Tomates	Tomatoes
Verano	Summer
Verduras	Vegetables

Barcos
Boats

Ancla	Anchor
Balsa	Raft
Boya	Buoy
Canoa	Canoe
Cuerda	Rope
Ferry	Ferry
Kayak	Kayak
Lago	Lake
Mar	Sea
Marea	Tide
Marinero	Sailor
Marítimo	Maritime
Mástil	Mast
Motor	Engine
Náutico	Nautical
Océano	Ocean
Río	River
Tripulación	Crew
Velero	Sailboat
Yate	Yacht

Belleza
Beauty

Aceites	Oils
Aroma	Scent
Champú	Shampoo
Color	Color
Cosméticos	Cosmetics
Elegancia	Elegance
Elegante	Elegant
Encanto	Charm
Espejo	Mirror
Estilista	Stylist
Fotogénico	Photogenic
Fragancia	Fragrance
Gracia	Grace
Maquillaje	Makeup
Piel	Skin
Pintalabios	Lipstick
Rizos	Curls
Rímel	Mascara
Servicios	Services
Tijeras	Scissors

Biología
Biology

Anatomía	Anatomy
Bacterias	Bacteria
Celda	Cell
Colágeno	Collagen
Cromosoma	Chromosome
Embrión	Embryo
Enzima	Enzyme
Evolución	Evolution
Hormona	Hormone
Mamífero	Mammal
Mutación	Mutation
Natural	Natural
Nervio	Nerve
Neurona	Neuron
Ósmosis	Osmosis
Plantas	Plants
Proteína	Protein
Reptil	Reptile
Simbiosis	Symbiosis
Sinapsis	Synapse

Boxeo
Boxing

Árbitro	Referee
Barbilla	Chin
Campana	Bell
Centrar	Focus
Codo	Elbow
Cuerdas	Ropes
Cuerpo	Body
Esquina	Corner
Exhausto	Exhausted
Fuerza	Strength
Guantes	Gloves
Habilidad	Skill
Lesiones	Injuries
Luchador	Fighter
Oponente	Opponent
Patear	Kick
Puntos	Points
Puño	Fist
Rápido	Quick
Recuperación	Recovery

Café
Coffee

Agua	Water
Amargo	Bitter
Aroma	Aroma
Asado	Roasted
Azúcar	Sugar
Ácido	Acidic
Bebida	Beverage
Cafeína	Caffeine
Crema	Cream
Filtro	Filter
Leche	Milk
Líquido	Liquid
Mañana	Morning
Moler	Grind
Negro	Black
Origen	Origin
Precio	Price
Sabor	Flavor
Taza	Cup
Variedad	Variety

Calentamiento Global
Global Warming

Ahora	Now
Ambiental	Environmental
Atención	Attention
Ártico	Arctic
Científico	Scientist
Clima	Climate
Consecuencias	Consequences
Crisis	Crisis
Datos	Data
Desarrollo	Development
Energía	Energy
Futuro	Future
Gas	Gas
Generaciones	Generations
Gobierno	Government
Industria	Industry
Internacional	International
Legislación	Legislation
Poblaciones	Populations
Temperaturas	Temperatures

Camping
Camping

Animales	Animals
Aventura	Adventure
Árboles	Trees
Bosque	Forest
Brújula	Compass
Cabina	Cabin
Canoa	Canoe
Caza	Hunting
Cuerda	Rope
Equipo	Equipment
Fuego	Fire
Hamaca	Hammock
Insecto	Insect
Lago	Lake
Linterna	Lantern
Luna	Moon
Mapa	Map
Montaña	Mountain
Naturaleza	Nature
Sombrero	Hat

Casa
House

Alfombra	Rug
Ático	Attic
Biblioteca	Library
Chimenea	Fireplace
Cocina	Kitchen
Dormitorio	Bedroom
Ducha	Shower
Escoba	Broom
Espejo	Mirror
Garaje	Garage
Grifo	Faucet
Jardín	Garden
Lámpara	Lamp
Pared	Wall
Piso	Floor
Puerta	Door
Sótano	Basement
Techo	Roof
Valla	Fence
Ventana	Window

Chocolate
Chocolate

Amargo	Bitter
Antioxidante	Antioxidant
Aroma	Aroma
Artesanal	Artisanal
Azúcar	Sugar
Cacahuetes	Peanuts
Cacao	Cacao
Calidad	Quality
Calorías	Calories
Caramelo	Caramel
Coco	Coconut
Delicioso	Delicious
Dulce	Sweet
Exótico	Exotic
Favorito	Favorite
Gusto	Taste
Ingrediente	Ingredient
Polvo	Powder
Receta	Recipe
Sabor	Flavor

Ciencia
Science

Átomo	Atom
Científico	Scientist
Clima	Climate
Datos	Data
Evolución	Evolution
Experimento	Experiment
Física	Physics
Fósil	Fossil
Gravedad	Gravity
Hecho	Fact
Hipótesis	Hypothesis
Laboratorio	Laboratory
Método	Method
Minerales	Minerals
Moléculas	Molecules
Naturaleza	Nature
Organismo	Organism
Partículas	Particles
Plantas	Plants
Químico	Chemical

Ciencia Ficción
Science Fiction

Atómico	Atomic
Cine	Cinema
Distante	Distant
Explosión	Explosion
Extremo	Extreme
Fantástico	Fantastic
Fuego	Fire
Futurista	Futuristic
Galaxia	Galaxy
Ilusión	Illusion
Imaginario	Imaginary
Libros	Books
Misterioso	Mysterious
Mundo	World
Oráculo	Oracle
Planeta	Planet
Realista	Realistic
Robots	Robots
Tecnología	Technology
Utopía	Utopia

Cocina
Kitchen

Caldera	Kettle
Comer	To Eat
Comida	Food
Congelador	Freezer
Cucharas	Spoons
Cucharón	Ladle
Cuchillos	Knives
Delantal	Apron
Especias	Spices
Esponja	Sponge
Horno	Oven
Jarra	Jug
Palillos	Chopsticks
Parrilla	Grill
Receta	Recipe
Refrigerador	Refrigerator
Servilleta	Napkin
Tazas	Cups
Tazón	Bowl
Tenedores	Forks

Colores
Colors

Amarillo	Yellow
Azul	Blue
Azur	Azure
Beige	Beige
Blanco	White
Carmesí	Crimson
Cian	Cyan
Fucsia	Fuchsia
Gris	Grey
Índigo	Indigo
Magenta	Magenta
Marrón	Brown
Naranja	Orange
Negro	Black
Púrpura	Purple
Rojo	Red
Rosa	Pink
Sepia	Sepia
Verde	Green
Violeta	Violet

Comida #1
Food #1

Ajo	Garlic
Albahaca	Basil
Atún	Tuna
Azúcar	Sugar
Canela	Cinnamon
Carne	Meat
Cebada	Barley
Cebolla	Onion
Ensalada	Salad
Espinacas	Spinach
Fresa	Strawberry
Jugo	Juice
Leche	Milk
Limón	Lemon
Menta	Mint
Nabo	Turnip
Pera	Pear
Sal	Salt
Sopa	Soup
Zanahoria	Carrot

Comida #2
Food #2

Alcachofa	Artichoke
Almendra	Almond
Apio	Celery
Arroz	Rice
Berenjena	Eggplant
Cereza	Cherry
Chocolate	Chocolate
Girasol	Sunflower
Huevo	Egg
Jengibre	Ginger
Kiwi	Kiwi
Manzana	Apple
Pan	Bread
Plátano	Banana
Pollo	Chicken
Queso	Cheese
Tomate	Tomato
Trigo	Wheat
Uva	Grape
Yogur	Yogurt

Conduciendo
Driving

Accidente	Accident
Autobús	Bus
Calle	Street
Camión	Truck
Coche	Car
Combustible	Fuel
Frenos	Brakes
Garaje	Garage
Gas	Gas
Licencia	License
Mapa	Map
Motocicleta	Motorcycle
Motor	Motor
Peatonal	Pedestrian
Peligro	Danger
Policía	Police
Seguridad	Safety
Tráfico	Traffic
Túnel	Tunnel
Velocidad	Speed

Creatividad
Creativity

Artístico	Artistic
Autenticidad	Authenticity
Claridad	Clarity
Dramático	Dramatic
Emociones	Emotions
Espontáneo	Spontaneous
Expresión	Expression
Fluidez	Fluidity
Habilidad	Skill
Ideas	Ideas
Imagen	Image
Imaginación	Imagination
Impresión	Impression
Inspiración	Inspiration
Intensidad	Intensity
Intuición	Intuition
Inventivo	Inventive
Sensación	Sensation
Visiones	Visions
Vitalidad	Vitality

Cuerpo Humano
Human Body

Barbilla	Chin
Boca	Mouth
Cabeza	Head
Cara	Face
Cerebro	Brain
Codo	Elbow
Corazón	Heart
Cuello	Neck
Dedo	Finger
Hombro	Shoulder
Lengua	Tongue
Mano	Hand
Nariz	Nose
Ojo	Eye
Oreja	Ear
Piel	Skin
Pierna	Leg
Rodilla	Knee
Sangre	Blood
Tobillo	Ankle

Deporte
Sport

Atleta	Athlete
Baile	Dancing
Capacidad	Ability
Ciclismo	Cycling
Cuerpo	Body
Deportes	Sports
Dieta	Diet
Entrenador	Coach
Estiramiento	Stretching
Fuerza	Strength
Huesos	Bones
Maximizar	Maximize
Metabólico	Metabolic
Músculos	Muscles
Nadar	To Swim
Nutrición	Nutrition
Programa	Program
Resistencia	Endurance
Respirar	To Breathe
Salud	Health

Diplomacia
Diplomacy

Asesor	Adviser
Comunidad	Community
Conflicto	Conflict
Cooperación	Cooperation
Diplomático	Diplomatic
Discusión	Discussion
Embajada	Embassy
Embajador	Ambassador
Extranjero	Foreign
Ética	Ethics
Gobierno	Government
Humanitario	Humanitarian
Idiomas	Languages
Integridad	Integrity
Justicia	Justice
Política	Politics
Resolución	Resolution
Seguridad	Security
Solución	Solution
Tratado	Treaty

Disciplinas Científicas
Scientific Disciplines

Anatomía	Anatomy
Arqueología	Archaeology
Astronomía	Astronomy
Biología	Biology
Bioquímica	Biochemistry
Botánica	Botany
Ecología	Ecology
Fisiología	Physiology
Geología	Geology
Inmunología	Immunology
Lingüística	Linguistics
Mecánica	Mechanics
Meteorología	Meteorology
Mineralogía	Mineralogy
Neurología	Neurology
Nutrición	Nutrition
Psicología	Psychology
Química	Chemistry
Sociología	Sociology
Zoología	Zoology

Días y Meses
Days and Months

Abril	April
Agosto	August
Año	Year
Calendario	Calendar
Domingo	Sunday
Enero	January
Febrero	February
Jueves	Thursday
Julio	July
Junio	June
Lunes	Monday
Martes	Tuesday
Mes	Month
Miércoles	Wednesday
Noviembre	November
Octubre	October
Sábado	Saturday
Semana	Week
Septiembre	September
Viernes	Friday

Ecología
Ecology

Clima	Climate
Comunidades	Communities
Diversidad	Diversity
Especie	Species
Fauna	Fauna
Flora	Flora
Global	Global
Hábitat	Habitat
Marino	Marine
Natural	Natural
Naturaleza	Nature
Pantano	Marsh
Plantas	Plants
Recursos	Resources
Sequía	Drought
Sostenible	Sustainable
Supervivencia	Survival
Variedad	Variety
Vegetación	Vegetation
Voluntarios	Volunteers

Edificios
Buildings

Albergue	Hostel
Apartamento	Apartment
Castillo	Castle
Cine	Cinema
Embajada	Embassy
Escuela	School
Estadio	Stadium
Fábrica	Factory
Garaje	Garage
Granero	Barn
Granja	Farm
Hospital	Hospital
Hotel	Hotel
Laboratorio	Laboratory
Museo	Museum
Observatorio	Observatory
Supermercado	Supermarket
Teatro	Theater
Torre	Tower
Universidad	University

Electricidad
Electricity

Almacenamiento	Storage
Batería	Battery
Bombilla	Bulb
Cable	Cable
Cables	Wires
Cantidad	Quantity
Electricista	Electrician
Eléctrico	Electric
Enchufe	Socket
Equipo	Equipment
Generador	Generator
Imán	Magnet
Lámpara	Lamp
Láser	Laser
Negativo	Negative
Objetos	Objects
Positivo	Positive
Red	Network
Televisión	Television
Teléfono	Telephone

Emociones
Emotions

Aburrimiento	Boredom
Agradecido	Grateful
Alegría	Joy
Alivio	Relief
Amor	Love
Avergonzado	Embarrassed
Beatitud	Bliss
Bondad	Kindness
Calma	Calm
Contenido	Content
Ira	Anger
Miedo	Fear
Paz	Peace
Relajado	Relaxed
Satisfecho	Satisfied
Simpatía	Sympathy
Sorpresa	Surprise
Ternura	Tenderness
Tranquilidad	Tranquility
Tristeza	Sadness

Energía
Energy

Batería	Battery
Calor	Heat
Carbono	Carbon
Combustible	Fuel
Contaminación	Pollution
Diesel	Diesel
Electrón	Electron
Eléctrico	Electric
Entropía	Entropy
Fotón	Photon
Gasolina	Gasoline
Hidrógeno	Hydrogen
Industria	Industry
Motor	Motor
Nuclear	Nuclear
Renovable	Renewable
Sol	Sun
Turbina	Turbine
Vapor	Steam
Viento	Wind

Enfermedad
Disease

Abdominal	Abdominal
Alergias	Allergies
Bienestar	Wellness
Contagioso	Contagious
Corazón	Heart
Crónica	Chronic
Cuerpo	Body
Débil	Weak
Genético	Genetic
Hereditario	Hereditary
Huesos	Bones
Inflamación	Inflammation
Inmunidad	Immunity
Lumbar	Lumbar
Neuropatía	Neuropathy
Pulmonar	Pulmonary
Respiratorio	Respiratory
Salud	Health
Síndrome	Syndrome
Terapia	Therapy

Especias
Spices

Agrio	Sour
Ajo	Garlic
Amargo	Bitter
Anís	Anise
Azafrán	Saffron
Canela	Cinnamon
Cebolla	Onion
Clavo	Clove
Comino	Cumin
Curry	Curry
Dulce	Sweet
Hinojo	Fennel
Jengibre	Ginger
Nuez Moscada	Nutmeg
Pimentón	Paprika
Pimienta	Pepper
Regaliz	Licorice
Sabor	Flavor
Sal	Salt
Vainilla	Vanilla

Ética
Ethics

Altruismo	Altruism
Bondad	Kindness
Compasión	Compassion
Cooperación	Cooperation
Dignidad	Dignity
Diplomático	Diplomatic
Filosofía	Philosophy
Honestidad	Honesty
Humanidad	Humanity
Individualismo	Individualism
Integridad	Integrity
Optimismo	Optimism
Paciencia	Patience
Racionalidad	Rationality
Razonable	Reasonable
Realismo	Realism
Respetuoso	Respectful
Sabiduría	Wisdom
Tolerancia	Tolerance
Valores	Values

Familia
Family

Abuela	Grandmother
Abuelo	Grandfather
Antepasado	Ancestor
Esposa	Wife
Hermana	Sister
Hermano	Brother
Hija	Daughter
Infancia	Childhood
Madre	Mother
Marido	Husband
Materno	Maternal
Nieto	Grandson
Niño	Child
Niños	Children
Padre	Father
Primo	Cousin
Sobrina	Niece
Sobrino	Nephew
Tía	Aunt
Tío	Uncle

Filantropía
Philanthropy

Caridad	Charity
Comunidad	Community
Contactos	Contacts
Donar	Donate
Finanzas	Finance
Fondos	Funds
Generosidad	Generosity
Gente	People
Global	Global
Grupos	Groups
Historia	History
Honestidad	Honesty
Humanidad	Humanity
Juventud	Youth
Metas	Goals
Misión	Mission
Necesitar	Need
Niños	Children
Programas	Programs
Público	Public

Física
Physics

Aceleración	Acceleration
Átomo	Atom
Caos	Chaos
Densidad	Density
Electrón	Electron
Fórmula	Formula
Frecuencia	Frequency
Gas	Gas
Gravedad	Gravity
Magnetismo	Magnetism
Masa	Mass
Mecánica	Mechanics
Molécula	Molecule
Motor	Engine
Nuclear	Nuclear
Partícula	Particle
Químico	Chemical
Relatividad	Relativity
Universal	Universal
Velocidad	Velocity

Flores
Flowers

Amapola	Poppy
Caléndula	Calendula
Diente de León	Dandelion
Gardenia	Gardenia
Girasol	Sunflower
Hibisco	Hibiscus
Jazmín	Jasmine
Lavanda	Lavender
Lila	Lilac
Lirio	Lily
Magnolia	Magnolia
Margarita	Daisy
Narciso	Daffodil
Orquídea	Orchid
Peonía	Peony
Pétalo	Petal
Ramo	Bouquet
Rosa	Rose
Trébol	Clover
Tulipán	Tulip

Formas
Shapes

Arco	Arc
Bordes	Edges
Cilindro	Cylinder
Círculo	Circle
Cono	Cone
Cuadrado	Square
Cubo	Cube
Curva	Curve
Elipse	Ellipse
Esfera	Sphere
Esquina	Corner
Hipérbola	Hyperbola
Lado	Side
Línea	Line
Oval	Oval
Pirámide	Pyramid
Polígono	Polygon
Prisma	Prism
Rectángulo	Rectangle
Triángulo	Triangle

Fruta
Fruit

Aguacate	Avocado
Albaricoque	Apricot
Baya	Berry
Cereza	Cherry
Coco	Coconut
Frambuesa	Raspberry
Guayaba	Guava
Kiwi	Kiwi
Limón	Lemon
Mango	Mango
Manzana	Apple
Melocotón	Peach
Melón	Melon
Naranja	Orange
Nectarina	Nectarine
Papaya	Papaya
Pera	Pear
Piña	Pineapple
Plátano	Banana
Uva	Grape

Fuerza y Gravedad
Force and Gravity

Centro	Center
Descubrimiento	Discovery
Dinámico	Dynamic
Distancia	Distance
Eje	Axis
Expansión	Expansion
Física	Physics
Fricción	Friction
Impacto	Impact
Magnetismo	Magnetism
Magnitud	Magnitude
Mecánica	Mechanics
Órbita	Orbit
Peso	Weight
Planetas	Planets
Presión	Pressure
Propiedades	Properties
Tiempo	Time
Universal	Universal
Velocidad	Speed

Geografía
Geography

Altitud	Altitude
Atlas	Atlas
Ciudad	City
Continente	Continent
Hemisferio	Hemisphere
Isla	Island
Latitud	Latitude
Longitud	Longitude
Mapa	Map
Mar	Sea
Meridiano	Meridian
Montaña	Mountain
Mundo	World
Norte	North
Oeste	West
País	Country
Región	Region
Río	River
Sur	South
Territorio	Territory

Geología
Geology

Ácido	Acid
Calcio	Calcium
Capa	Layer
Caverna	Cavern
Continente	Continent
Coral	Coral
Cristales	Crystals
Cuarzo	Quartz
Erosión	Erosion
Estalactita	Stalactite
Estalagmitas	Stalagmites
Fósil	Fossil
Géiser	Geyser
Lava	Lava
Meseta	Plateau
Minerales	Minerals
Piedra	Stone
Sal	Salt
Terremoto	Earthquake
Volcán	Volcano

Geometría
Geometry

Altura	Height
Ángulo	Angle
Cálculo	Calculation
Curva	Curve
Diámetro	Diameter
Dimensión	Dimension
Ecuación	Equation
Horizontal	Horizontal
Lógica	Logic
Masa	Mass
Mediana	Median
Número	Number
Paralelo	Parallel
Proporción	Proportion
Segmento	Segment
Simetría	Symmetry
Superficie	Surface
Teoría	Theory
Triángulo	Triangle
Vertical	Vertical

Gobierno
Government

Ciudadanía	Citizenship
Civil	Civil
Constitución	Constitution
Democracia	Democracy
Discurso	Speech
Discusión	Discussion
Distrito	District
Estado	State
Igualdad	Equality
Independencia	Independence
Judicial	Judicial
Justicia	Justice
Ley	Law
Libertad	Liberty
Líder	Leader
Monumento	Monument
Nacional	National
Nación	Nation
Política	Politics
Símbolo	Symbol

Granja #1
Farm #1

Abeja	Bee
Agricultura	Agriculture
Agua	Water
Arroz	Rice
Burro	Donkey
Caballo	Horse
Cabra	Goat
Campo	Field
Cuervo	Crow
Fertilizante	Fertilizer
Gato	Cat
Heno	Hay
Miel	Honey
Perro	Dog
Pollo	Chicken
Semillas	Seeds
Ternero	Calf
Tierra	Land
Vaca	Cow
Valla	Fence

Granja #2
Farm #2

Agricultor	Farmer
Animales	Animals
Cebada	Barley
Colmena	Beehive
Comida	Food
Cordero	Lamb
Fruta	Fruit
Granero	Barn
Huerto	Orchard
Leche	Milk
Llama	Llama
Maíz	Corn
Oveja	Sheep
Pastor	Shepherd
Pato	Duck
Prado	Meadow
Riego	Irrigation
Tractor	Tractor
Trigo	Wheat
Vegetal	Vegetable

Herboristería
Herbalism

Ajo	Garlic
Albahaca	Basil
Aromático	Aromatic
Azafrán	Saffron
Calidad	Quality
Culinario	Culinary
Eneldo	Dill
Estragón	Tarragon
Flor	Flower
Hinojo	Fennel
Ingrediente	Ingredient
Jardín	Garden
Lavanda	Lavender
Mejorana	Marjoram
Menta	Mint
Perejil	Parsley
Planta	Plant
Romero	Rosemary
Sabor	Flavor
Verde	Green

Ingeniería
Engineering

Ángulo	Angle
Cálculo	Calculation
Construcción	Construction
Diagrama	Diagram
Diámetro	Diameter
Diesel	Diesel
Distribución	Distribution
Eje	Axis
Energía	Energy
Estabilidad	Stability
Estructura	Structure
Fricción	Friction
Fuerza	Strength
Líquido	Liquid
Máquina	Machine
Medición	Measurement
Motor	Motor
Palancas	Levers
Profundidad	Depth
Propulsión	Propulsion

Insectos
Insects

Abeja	Bee
Avispa	Wasp
Avispón	Hornet
Áfido	Aphid
Cigarra	Cicada
Cucaracha	Cockroach
Escarabajo	Beetle
Gusano	Worm
Hormiga	Ant
Langosta	Locust
Larva	Larva
Libélula	Dragonfly
Mantis	Mantis
Mariposa	Butterfly
Mariquita	Ladybug
Mosquito	Mosquito
Polilla	Moth
Pulga	Flea
Saltamontes	Grasshopper
Termita	Termite

Instrumentos Musicales
Musical Instruments

Armónica	Harmonica
Arpa	Harp
Banjo	Banjo
Clarinete	Clarinet
Fagot	Bassoon
Flauta	Flute
Gong	Gong
Guitarra	Guitar
Mandolina	Mandolin
Marimba	Marimba
Oboe	Oboe
Pandereta	Tambourine
Percusión	Percussion
Piano	Piano
Saxofón	Saxophone
Tambor	Drum
Trombón	Trombone
Trompeta	Trumpet
Violín	Violin
Violonchelo	Cello

Jardinería
Gardening

Agua	Water
Botánico	Botanical
Clima	Climate
Comestible	Edible
Compost	Compost
Contenedor	Container
Especie	Species
Estacional	Seasonal
Exótico	Exotic
Flor	Blossom
Floral	Floral
Follaje	Foliage
Hoja	Leaf
Huerto	Orchard
Humedad	Moisture
Manguera	Hose
Ramo	Bouquet
Semillas	Seeds
Suciedad	Dirt
Suelo	Soil

Jardín
Garden

Arbusto	Bush
Árbol	Tree
Banco	Bench
Césped	Lawn
Estanque	Pond
Flor	Flower
Garaje	Garage
Hamaca	Hammock
Hierba	Grass
Huerto	Orchard
Jardín	Garden
Malezas	Weeds
Manguera	Hose
Pala	Shovel
Porche	Porch
Rastrillo	Rake
Suelo	Soil
Terraza	Terrace
Trampolín	Trampoline
Valla	Fence

Jazz
Jazz

Artista	Artist
Álbum	Album
Canción	Song
Composición	Composition
Compositor	Composer
Concierto	Concert
Estilo	Style
Énfasis	Emphasis
Famoso	Famous
Favoritos	Favorites
Género	Genre
Improvisación	Improvisation
Música	Music
Nuevo	New
Orquesta	Orchestra
Ritmo	Rhythm
Talento	Talent
Tambores	Drums
Técnica	Technique
Viejo	Old

Libros
Books

Autor	Author
Aventura	Adventure
Colección	Collection
Contexto	Context
Dualidad	Duality
Escrito	Written
Historia	Story
Histórico	Historical
Humorístico	Humorous
Inventivo	Inventive
Lector	Reader
Literario	Literary
Narrador	Narrator
Novela	Novel
Página	Page
Pertinente	Relevant
Poema	Poem
Poesía	Poetry
Serie	Series
Trágico	Tragic

Literatura
Literature

Analogía	Analogy
Análisis	Analysis
Anécdota	Anecdote
Autor	Author
Biografía	Biography
Comparación	Comparison
Conclusión	Conclusion
Descripción	Description
Diálogo	Dialogue
Estilo	Style
Ficción	Fiction
Metáfora	Metaphor
Narrador	Narrator
Novela	Novel
Poema	Poem
Poético	Poetic
Rima	Rhyme
Ritmo	Rhythm
Tema	Theme
Tragedia	Tragedy

Mamíferos
Mammals

Ballena	Whale
Burro	Donkey
Caballo	Horse
Camello	Camel
Canguro	Kangaroo
Cebra	Zebra
Conejo	Rabbit
Coyote	Coyote
Delfín	Dolphin
Elefante	Elephant
Gato	Cat
Gorila	Gorilla
Jirafa	Giraffe
Lobo	Wolf
Mono	Monkey
Oso	Bear
Oveja	Sheep
Perro	Dog
Toro	Bull
Zorro	Fox

Matemáticas
Math

Aritmética	Arithmetic
Ángulos	Angles
Circunferencia	Circumference
Decimal	Decimal
Diámetro	Diameter
Ecuación	Equation
Esfera	Sphere
Exponente	Exponent
Fracción	Fraction
Geometría	Geometry
Paralelo	Parallel
Paralelogramo	Parallelogram
Perímetro	Perimeter
Perpendicular	Perpendicular
Polígono	Polygon
Radio	Radius
Rectángulo	Rectangle
Simetría	Symmetry
Triángulo	Triangle
Volumen	Volume

Mediciones
Measurements

Altura	Height
Ancho	Width
Byte	Byte
Centímetro	Centimeter
Decimal	Decimal
Grado	Degree
Gramo	Gram
Kilogramo	Kilogram
Kilómetro	Kilometer
Litro	Liter
Longitud	Length
Masa	Mass
Metro	Meter
Minuto	Minute
Onza	Ounce
Peso	Weight
Profundidad	Depth
Pulgada	Inch
Tonelada	Ton
Volumen	Volume

Meditación
Meditation

Aceptación	Acceptance
Atención	Attention
Bondad	Kindness
Calma	Calm
Claridad	Clarity
Compasión	Compassion
Emociones	Emotions
Gratitud	Gratitude
Mental	Mental
Mente	Mind
Movimiento	Movement
Música	Music
Naturaleza	Nature
Observación	Observation
Paz	Peace
Pensamientos	Thoughts
Perspectiva	Perspective
Postura	Posture
Respiración	Breathing
Silencio	Silence

Mitología
Mythology

Arquetipo	Archetype
Celos	Jealousy
Cielo	Heaven
Comportamiento	Behavior
Creación	Creation
Creencias	Beliefs
Criatura	Creature
Cultura	Culture
Desastre	Disaster
Fuerza	Strength
Guerrero	Warrior
Héroe	Hero
Inmortalidad	Immortality
Laberinto	Labyrinth
Leyenda	Legend
Monstruo	Monster
Mortal	Mortal
Rayo	Lightning
Trueno	Thunder
Venganza	Revenge

Moda
Fashion

Bordado	Embroidery
Botones	Buttons
Boutique	Boutique
Caro	Expensive
Elegante	Elegant
Encaje	Lace
Estilo	Style
Mediciones	Measurements
Minimalista	Minimalist
Moderno	Modern
Modesto	Modest
Original	Original
Patrón	Pattern
Práctico	Practical
Ropa	Clothing
Sencillo	Simple
Sofisticado	Sophisticated
Tejido	Fabric
Tendencia	Trend
Textura	Texture

Mueble
Furniture

Alfombra	Rug
Almohada	Pillow
Armario	Armoire
Banco	Bench
Cama	Bed
Cojines	Cushions
Colchón	Mattress
Cortinas	Curtains
Cómoda	Dresser
Edredones	Comforters
Escritorio	Desk
Espejo	Mirror
Estantería	Bookcase
Estantes	Shelves
Futón	Futon
Hamaca	Hammock
Lámpara	Lamp
Silla	Chair
Sillón	Armchair
Sofá	Couch

Música
Music

Armonía	Harmony
Armónico	Harmonic
Álbum	Album
Balada	Ballad
Cantante	Singer
Cantar	Sing
Clásico	Classical
Coro	Chorus
Grabación	Recording
Improvisar	Improvise
Instrumento	Instrument
Melodía	Melody
Micrófono	Microphone
Musical	Musical
Músico	Musician
Ópera	Opera
Poético	Poetic
Ritmo	Rhythm
Tempo	Tempo
Vocal	Vocal

Naturaleza
Nature

Abejas	Bees
Animales	Animals
Ártico	Arctic
Belleza	Beauty
Bosque	Forest
Desierto	Desert
Dinámico	Dynamic
Erosión	Erosion
Follaje	Foliage
Glaciar	Glacier
Niebla	Fog
Nubes	Clouds
Pacífico	Peaceful
Refugio	Shelter
Río	River
Salvaje	Wild
Santuario	Sanctuary
Sereno	Serene
Tropical	Tropical
Vital	Vital

Negocio
Business

Carrera	Career
Costo	Cost
Descuento	Discount
Dinero	Money
Economía	Economics
Empleado	Employee
Empleador	Employer
Empresa	Company
Fábrica	Factory
Finanzas	Finance
Impuestos	Taxes
Inversión	Investment
Mercancía	Merchandise
Moneda	Currency
Oficina	Office
Presupuesto	Budget
Tienda	Shop
Trabajo	Job
Transacción	Transaction
Venta	Sale

Nutrición
Nutrition

Amargo	Bitter
Apetito	Appetite
Calidad	Quality
Calorías	Calories
Carbohidratos	Carbohydrates
Cereales	Cereals
Comestible	Edible
Dieta	Diet
Digestión	Digestion
Equilibrado	Balanced
Fermentación	Fermentation
Nutriente	Nutrient
Peso	Weight
Proteínas	Proteins
Sabor	Flavor
Salsa	Sauce
Salud	Health
Saludable	Healthy
Toxina	Toxin
Vitamina	Vitamin

Números
Numbers

Catorce	Fourteen
Cero	Zero
Cinco	Five
Cuatro	Four
Decimal	Decimal
Diecinueve	Nineteen
Dieciocho	Eighteen
Dieciséis	Sixteen
Diecisiete	Seventeen
Diez	Ten
Doce	Twelve
Dos	Two
Nueve	Nine
Ocho	Eight
Quince	Fifteen
Seis	Six
Siete	Seven
Trece	Thirteen
Tres	Three
Veinte	Twenty

Océano
Ocean

Alga	Algae
Anguila	Eel
Arrecife	Reef
Atún	Tuna
Ballena	Whale
Barco	Boat
Camarón	Shrimp
Cangrejo	Crab
Coral	Coral
Delfín	Dolphin
Esponja	Sponge
Mareas	Tides
Medusa	Jellyfish
Ostra	Oyster
Pescado	Fish
Pulpo	Octopus
Sal	Salt
Tiburón	Shark
Tormenta	Storm
Tortuga	Turtle

Paisajes
Landscapes

Cascada	Waterfall
Cueva	Cave
Desierto	Desert
Estuario	Estuary
Géiser	Geyser
Glaciar	Glacier
Iceberg	Iceberg
Isla	Island
Lago	Lake
Laguna	Lagoon
Mar	Sea
Montaña	Mountain
Oasis	Oasis
Pantano	Swamp
Península	Peninsula
Playa	Beach
Río	River
Tundra	Tundra
Valle	Valley
Volcán	Volcano

Países #1
Countries #1

Alemania	Germany
Argentina	Argentina
Bélgica	Belgium
Brasil	Brazil
Canadá	Canada
Ecuador	Ecuador
Egipto	Egypt
España	Spain
Filipinas	Philippines
Honduras	Honduras
India	India
Italia	Italy
Libia	Libya
Malí	Mali
Marruecos	Morocco
Nicaragua	Nicaragua
Noruega	Norway
Panamá	Panama
Polonia	Poland
Venezuela	Venezuela

Países #2
Countries #2

Albania	Albania
Australia	Australia
Austria	Austria
Dinamarca	Denmark
Etiopía	Ethiopia
Francia	France
Grecia	Greece
Indonesia	Indonesia
Irlanda	Ireland
Jamaica	Jamaica
Japón	Japan
Laos	Laos
México	Mexico
Pakistán	Pakistan
Portugal	Portugal
Rusia	Russia
Siria	Syria
Sudán	Sudan
Ucrania	Ukraine
Uganda	Uganda

Pájaros
Birds

Avestruz	Ostrich
Águila	Eagle
Cigüeña	Stork
Cisne	Swan
Cuco	Cuckoo
Cuervo	Crow
Flamenco	Flamingo
Ganso	Goose
Garza	Heron
Gaviota	Gull
Gorrión	Sparrow
Halcón	Hawk
Huevo	Egg
Loro	Parrot
Paloma	Pigeon
Pato	Duck
Pelícano	Pelican
Pingüino	Penguin
Pollo	Chicken
Tucán	Toucan

Plantas
Plants

Arbusto	Bush
Árbol	Tree
Bambú	Bamboo
Baya	Berry
Bosque	Forest
Botánica	Botany
Cactus	Cactus
Fertilizante	Fertilizer
Flor	Flower
Flora	Flora
Follaje	Foliage
Frijol	Bean
Hiedra	Ivy
Hierba	Grass
Hoja	Leaf
Jardín	Garden
Musgo	Moss
Pétalo	Petal
Raíz	Root
Vegetación	Vegetation

Profesiones #1
Professions #1

Abogado	Attorney
Astrónomo	Astronomer
Atleta	Athlete
Bailarín	Dancer
Banquero	Banker
Bombero	Firefighter
Cartógrafo	Cartographer
Cazador	Hunter
Doctor	Doctor
Editor	Editor
Embajador	Ambassador
Enfermera	Nurse
Entrenador	Coach
Fontanero	Plumber
Geólogo	Geologist
Joyero	Jeweler
Músico	Musician
Pianista	Pianist
Psicólogo	Psychologist
Veterinario	Veterinarian

Profesiones #2
Professions #2

Astronauta	Astronaut
Bibliotecario	Librarian
Biólogo	Biologist
Cirujano	Surgeon
Dentista	Dentist
Detective	Detective
Filósofo	Philosopher
Fotógrafo	Photographer
Ilustrador	Illustrator
Ingeniero	Engineer
Inventor	Inventor
Investigador	Researcher
Jardinero	Gardener
Lingüista	Linguist
Médico	Physician
Periodista	Journalist
Piloto	Pilot
Pintor	Painter
Profesor	Teacher
Zoólogo	Zoologist

Psicología
Psychology

Cita	Appointment
Clínico	Clinical
Cognición	Cognition
Comportamiento	Behavior
Conflicto	Conflict
Ego	Ego
Emociones	Emotions
Evaluación	Assessment
Ideas	Ideas
Inconsciente	Unconscious
Infancia	Childhood
Pensamientos	Thoughts
Percepción	Perception
Personalidad	Personality
Problema	Problem
Realidad	Reality
Sensación	Sensation
Subconsciente	Subconscious
Sueños	Dreams
Terapia	Therapy

Química
Chemistry

Alcalino	Alkaline
Ácido	Acid
Calor	Heat
Carbono	Carbon
Catalizador	Catalyst
Cloro	Chlorine
Electrón	Electron
Enzima	Enzyme
Gas	Gas
Hidrógeno	Hydrogen
Ion	Ion
Líquido	Liquid
Metales	Metals
Molécula	Molecule
Nuclear	Nuclear
Oxígeno	Oxygen
Peso	Weight
Reacción	Reaction
Sal	Salt
Temperatura	Temperature

Restaurante #1
Restaurant #1

Alergia	Allergy
Café	Coffee
Cajero	Cashier
Camarera	Waitress
Carne	Meat
Cocina	Kitchen
Comer	To Eat
Comida	Food
Cuchillo	Knife
Ingredientes	Ingredients
Menú	Menu
Pan	Bread
Picante	Spicy
Plato	Plate
Pollo	Chicken
Postre	Dessert
Reserva	Reservation
Salsa	Sauce
Servilleta	Napkin
Tazón	Bowl

Restaurante #2
Restaurant #2

Agua	Water
Almuerzo	Lunch
Aperitivo	Appetizer
Bebida	Beverage
Camarero	Waiter
Cena	Dinner
Cuchara	Spoon
Delicioso	Delicious
Ensalada	Salad
Especias	Spices
Fruta	Fruit
Hielo	Ice
Huevos	Eggs
Pastel	Cake
Pescado	Fish
Sal	Salt
Silla	Chair
Sopa	Soup
Tenedor	Fork
Verduras	Vegetables

Ropa
Clothes

Abrigo	Coat
Blusa	Blouse
Bufanda	Scarf
Camisa	Shirt
Chaqueta	Jacket
Cinturón	Belt
Collar	Necklace
Delantal	Apron
Falda	Skirt
Guantes	Gloves
Joyas	Jewelry
Moda	Fashion
Pantalones	Pants
Pijama	Pajamas
Pulsera	Bracelet
Sandalias	Sandals
Sombrero	Hat
Suéter	Sweater
Vestido	Dress
Zapato	Shoe

Salud y Bienestar #1
Health and Wellness #1

Activo	Active
Altura	Height
Bacterias	Bacteria
Clínica	Clinic
Doctor	Doctor
Farmacia	Pharmacy
Fractura	Fracture
Hambre	Hunger
Hábito	Habit
Hormonas	Hormones
Huesos	Bones
Medicina	Medicine
Músculos	Muscles
Piel	Skin
Postura	Posture
Reflejo	Reflex
Relajación	Relaxation
Terapia	Therapy
Tratamiento	Treatment
Virus	Virus

Salud y Bienestar #2
Health and Wellness #2

Alergia	Allergy
Anatomía	Anatomy
Apetito	Appetite
Caloría	Calorie
Dieta	Diet
Digestión	Digestion
Energía	Energy
Enfermedad	Disease
Estrés	Stress
Genética	Genetics
Higiene	Hygiene
Hospital	Hospital
Infección	Infection
Masaje	Massage
Nutrición	Nutrition
Peso	Weight
Recuperación	Recovery
Saludable	Healthy
Sangre	Blood
Vitamina	Vitamin

Selva Tropical
Rainforest

Anfibios	Amphibians
Botánico	Botanical
Clima	Climate
Comunidad	Community
Diversidad	Diversity
Especie	Species
Indígena	Indigenous
Insectos	Insects
Mamíferos	Mammals
Musgo	Moss
Naturaleza	Nature
Nubes	Clouds
Pájaros	Birds
Preservación	Preservation
Refugio	Refuge
Respeto	Respect
Restauración	Restoration
Selva	Jungle
Supervivencia	Survival
Valioso	Valuable

Senderismo
Hiking

Acantilado	Cliff
Agua	Water
Animales	Animals
Botas	Boots
Camping	Camping
Cansado	Tired
Clima	Climate
Cumbre	Summit
Guías	Guides
Mapa	Map
Montaña	Mountain
Mosquitos	Mosquitoes
Naturaleza	Nature
Orientación	Orientation
Parques	Parks
Pesado	Heavy
Piedras	Stones
Preparación	Preparation
Salvaje	Wild
Sol	Sun

Suministros de Arte
Art Supplies

Aceite	Oil
Acrílico	Acrylic
Acuarelas	Watercolors
Agua	Water
Arcilla	Clay
Borrador	Eraser
Caballete	Easel
Cámara	Camera
Cepillos	Brushes
Colores	Colors
Creatividad	Creativity
Ideas	Ideas
Lápices	Pencils
Mesa	Table
Papel	Paper
Pasteles	Pastels
Pegamento	Glue
Pinturas	Paints
Silla	Chair
Tinta	Ink

Tipos de Cabello
Hair Types

Blanco	White
Brillante	Shiny
Calvo	Bald
Corto	Short
Delgada	Thin
Gris	Gray
Grueso	Thick
Largo	Long
Marrón	Brown
Negro	Black
Ondulado	Wavy
Plata	Silver
Rizado	Curly
Rizos	Curls
Rubio	Blond
Saludable	Healthy
Seco	Dry
Suave	Soft
Trenzado	Braided
Trenzas	Braids

Enhorabuena

Lo has conseguido!

Esperamos que hayas disfrutado de este libro tanto como nosotros al diseñarlo. Nos esforzamos por crear libros de la máxima calidad posible.
Esta edición está diseñada para proporcionar un aprendizaje inteligente, de calidad y divertido!

¿Te ha gustado este libro?

Una Petición Sencilla

Estos libros existen gracias a las reseñas que se publican.
¿Podrías ayudarnos dejando una reseña ahora?
Aquí tienes un breve enlace a la página de reseñas

BestBooksActivity.com/Opiniones50

¡DESAFÍO FINAL!

Reto n°1

¿Estás listo para tu juego gratis? Los utilizamos siempre, pero no son tan fáciles de encontrar. ¡Aquí están los **Sinónimos**!
Escribe 5 palabras que hayas encontrado en los rompecabezas (#21, #36, #76) y trata de encontrar 2 sinónimos para cada palabra.

Escriba 5 palabras del **Puzzle 21**

Palabras	Sinónimo 1	Sinónimo 2

Escriba 5 palabras del **Puzzle 36**

Palabras	Sinónimo 1	Sinónimo 2

Escriba 5 palabras del **Puzzle 76**

Palabras	Sinónimo 1	Sinónimo 2

Reto n°2

Ahora que te has calentado, escribe 5 palabras que hayas encontrado en los Puzzles 9, 17 y 25 e intenta encontrar 2 antónimos para cada palabra. ¿Cuántos puedes encontrar en 20 minutos?

Escriba 5 palabras del **Puzzle 9**

Palabras	Antónimo 1	Antónimo 2

Escriba 5 palabras del **Puzzle 17**

Palabras	Antónimo 1	Antónimo 2

Escriba 5 palabras del **Puzzle 25**

Palabras	Antónimo 1	Antónimo 2

Reto n°3

¡Genial! Este desafío final no es nada para ti.

¿Preparado para el reto final? Elige 10 palabras que hayas descubierto en los diferentes rompecabezas y escríbelas a continuación.

1.	6.
2.	7.
3.	8.
4.	9.
5.	10.

Ahora escribe un texto pensando en una persona, un animal o un lugar que te guste.

Puedes usar la última página de este libro como borrador.

Tu Composición:

CUADERNO DE NOTAS :

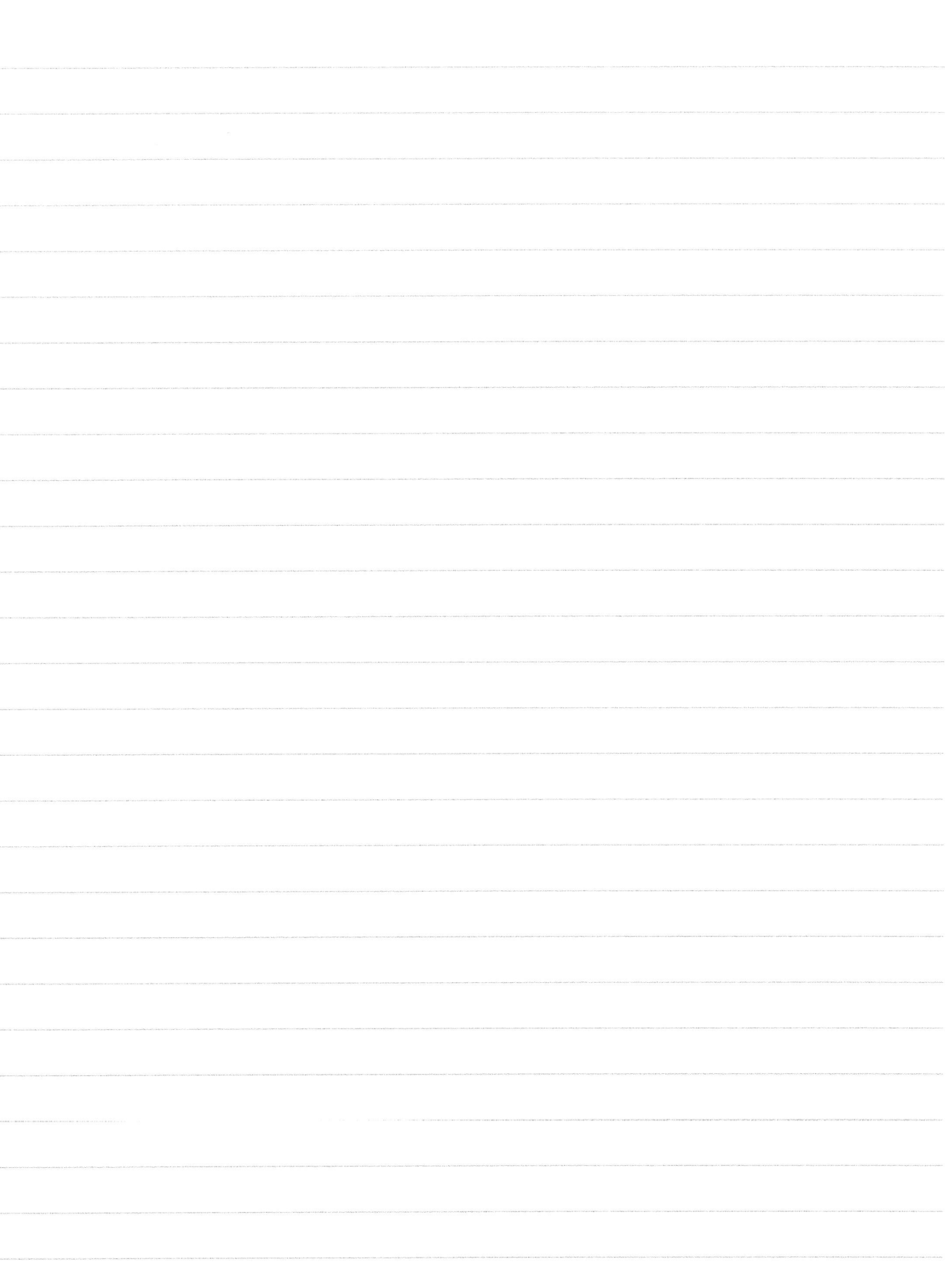

HASTA PRONTO !

Todo el Equipo

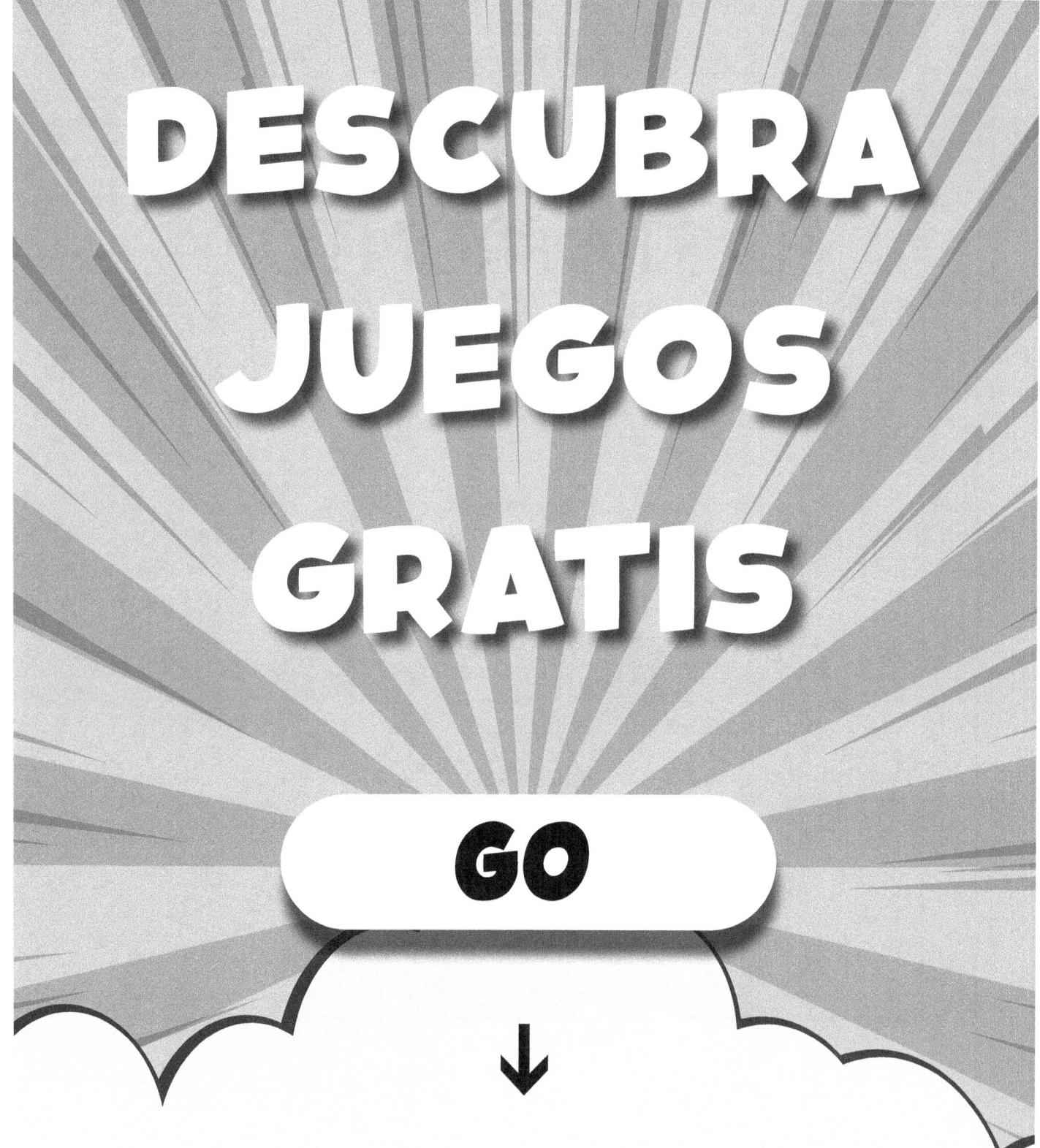

BESTACTIVITYBOOKS.COM/FREEGAMES